The Grown-Ups Coloring Book
Through the Looking Glass

A Series of Adult Coloring Books featuring Alice in Through the Looking Glass. Volume 5 illustrations are for reducing stress, relaxation, entertainment, creativity, happiness, tranquility and sharpening of the mind.

Volume 5

by

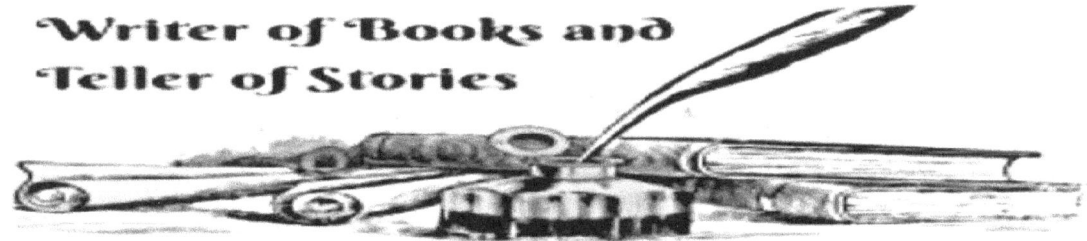

Writer of Books and
Teller of Stories

RonaldHudkins.com

Copyright Notice

Book Index Table of Contents

Book Description

Through the Looking Glass and what Alice found there. This is an 1871 novel written by English author Charles Lutwidge Dodgson under the pseudonym Lewis Carroll. It is a sequel to Alice's adventures in Wonderland (1865). Set six months later than the earlier book, Alice again enters a fantastical world, this time by climbing through a mirror into a world that she can see beyond it.

The forty plus book illustrations in this fifth addition series of Grown-Up Coloring Books is the original art of Sir John Tenniel. English Golden Age Illustrator (1820- 1941). This is the artist who originally illustrated both Lewis Carrol's Alice's Adventures in Wonderland and the illustrations contained in this book titled Through the Looking Glass.

Celebrating the 149th anniversary of Alice's Adventures Through the Looking Glass comes this richly illustrated Adult Coloring Book. So now, it is time for you to begin your coloring journey and release your creative abilities upon Tweedledee, Red Queen, White Knight and Jabberwock to say nothing of the immortal young Alice and others. Have fun and enjoy!

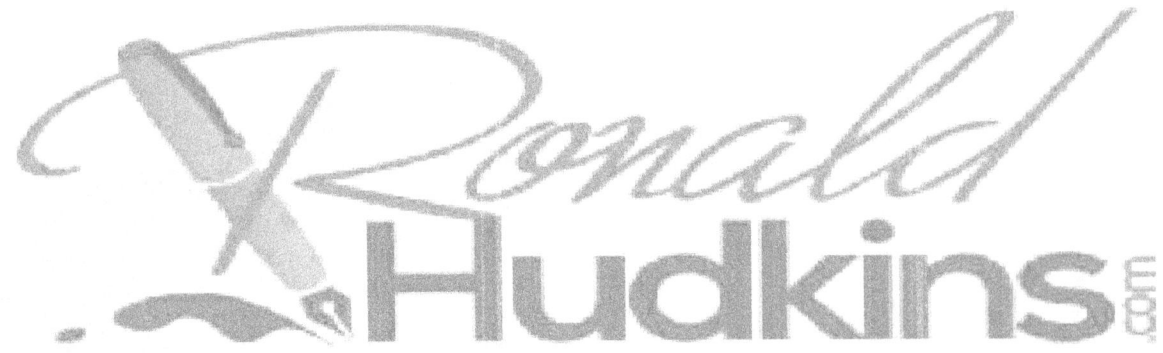

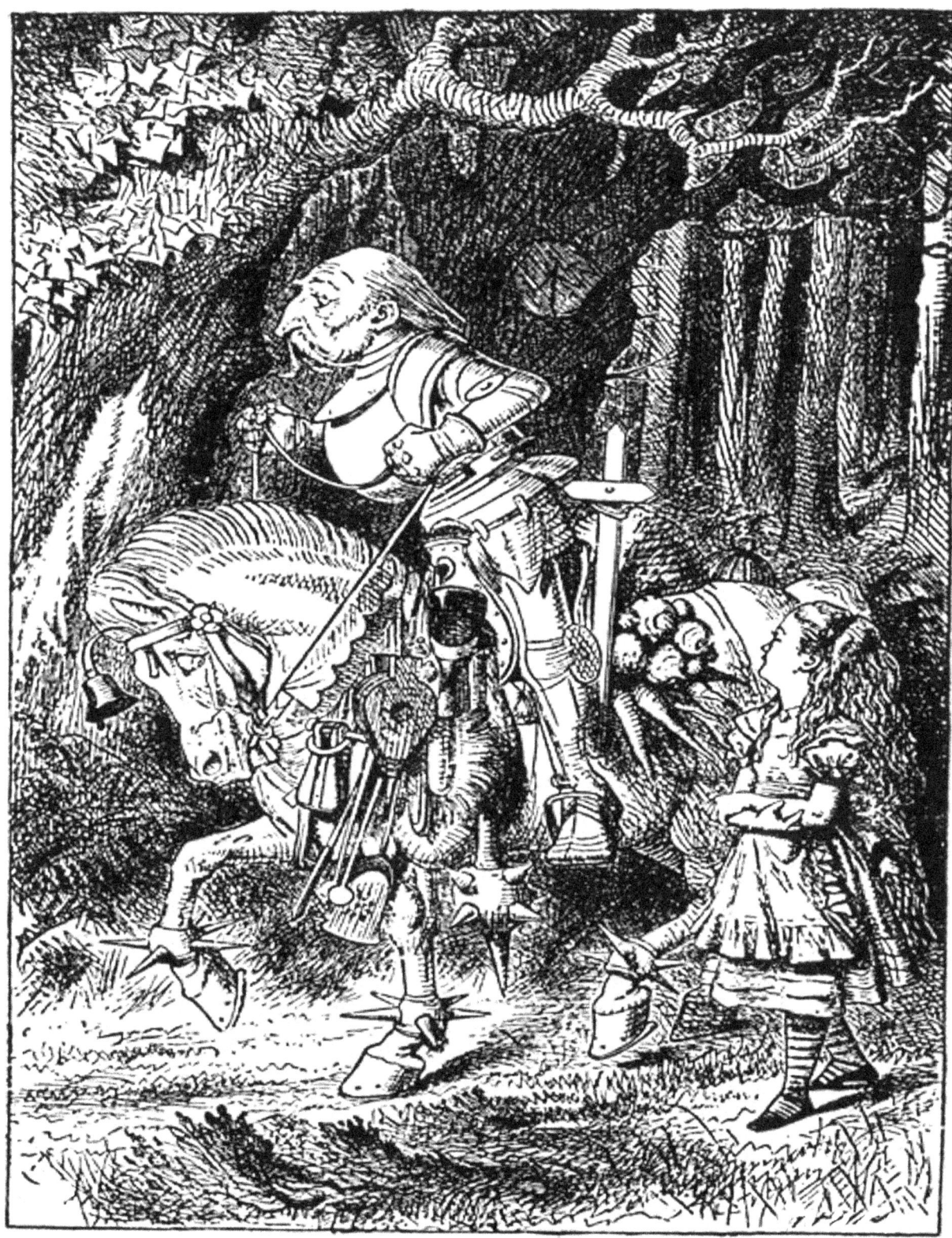

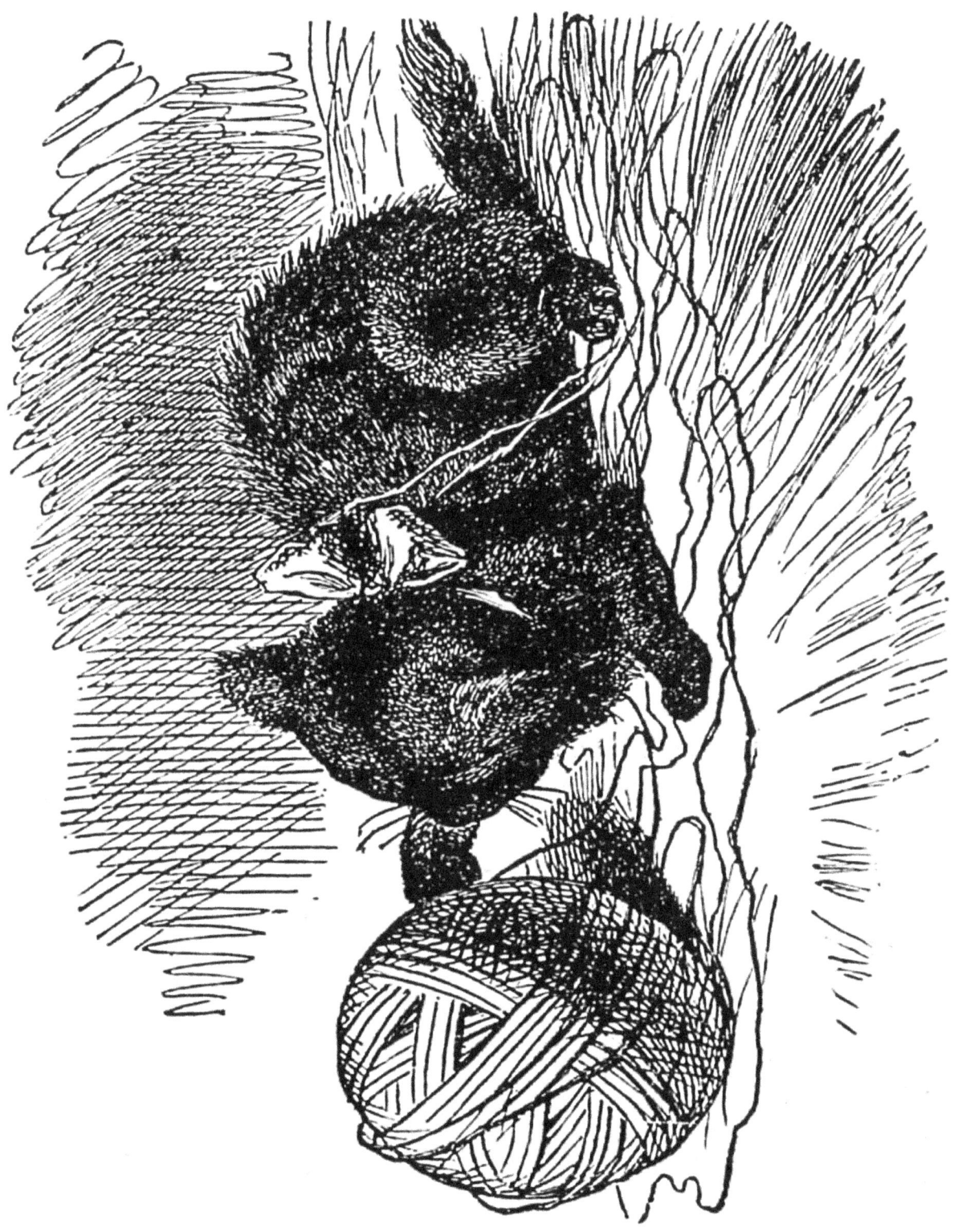

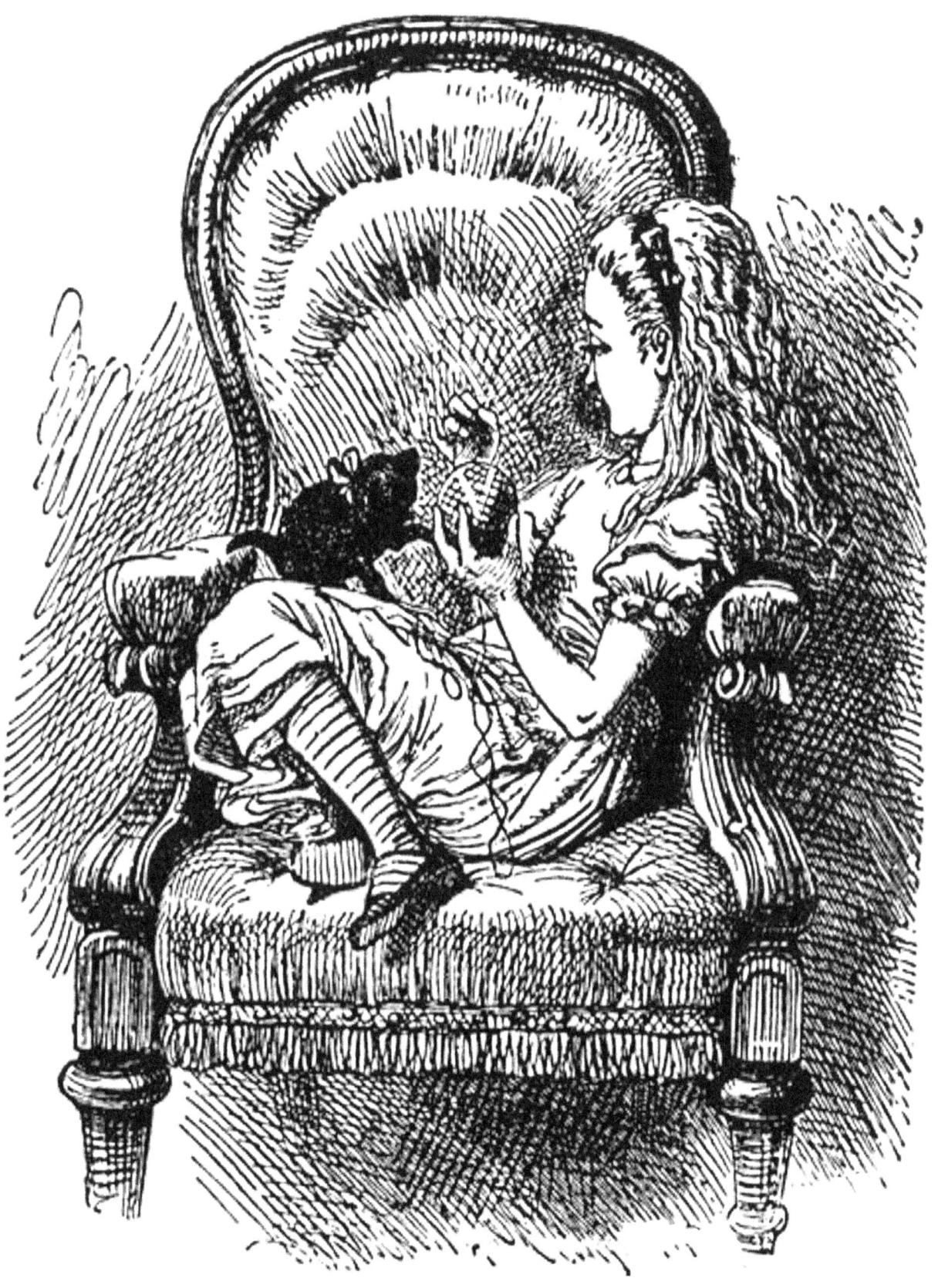

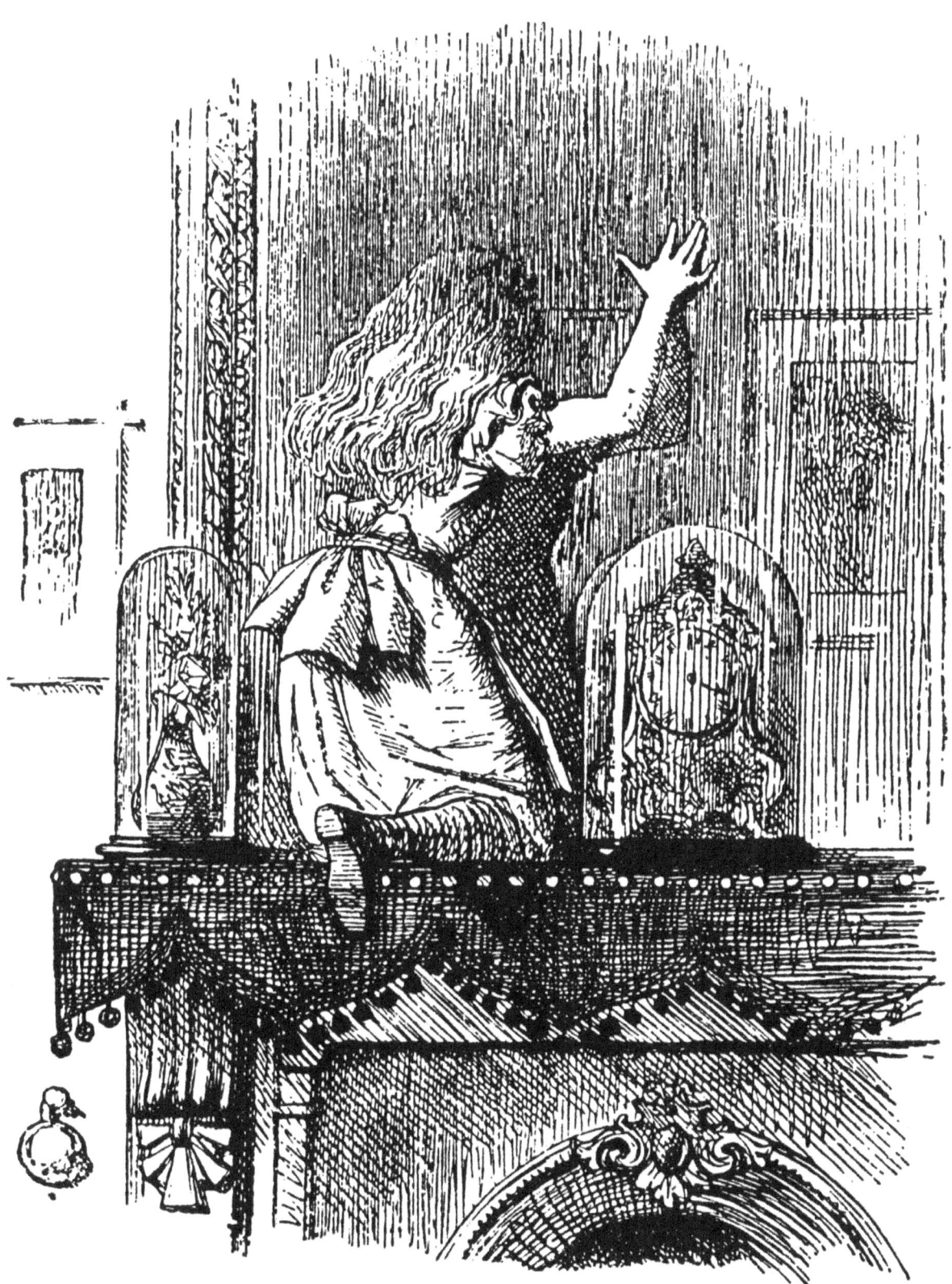

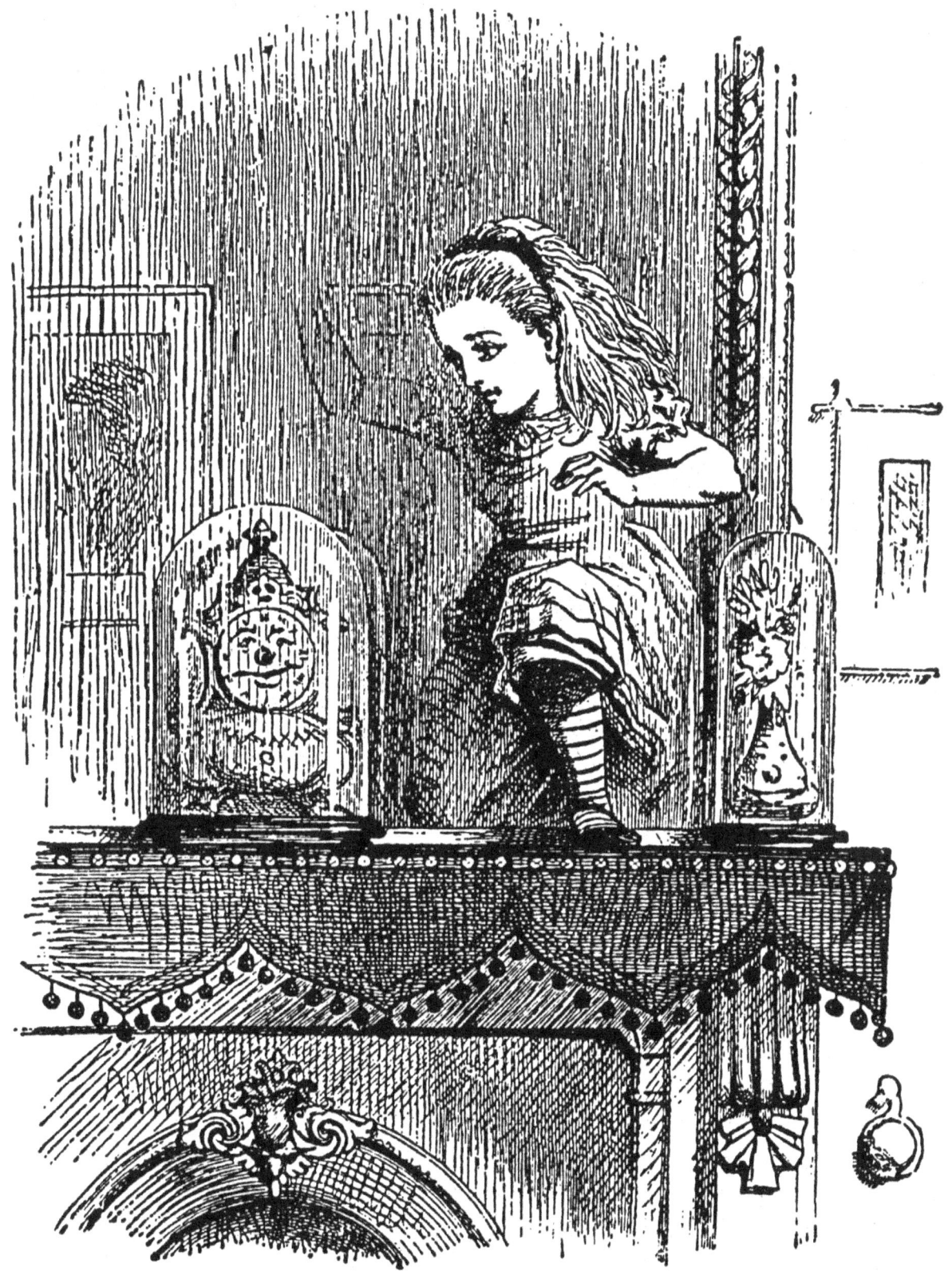

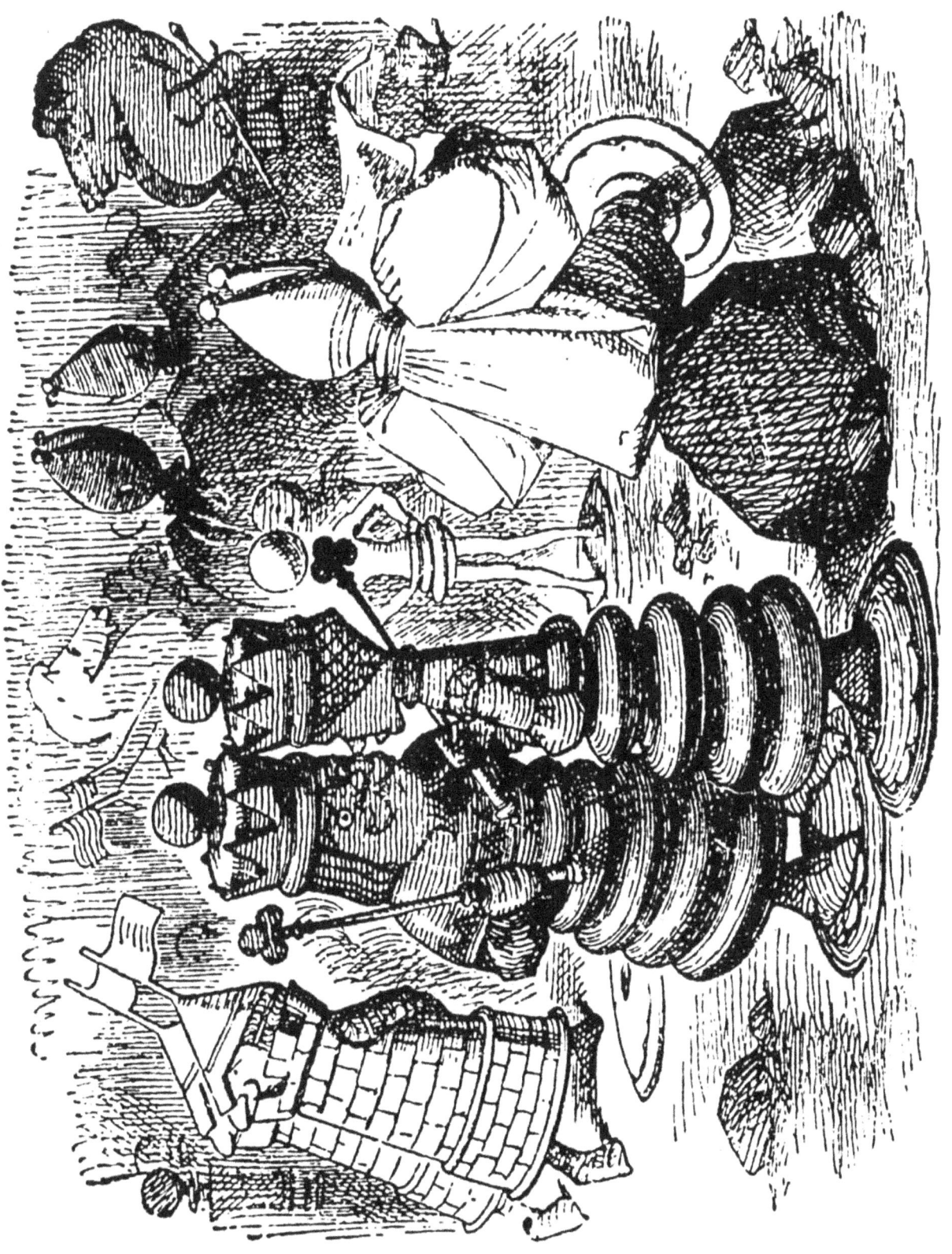

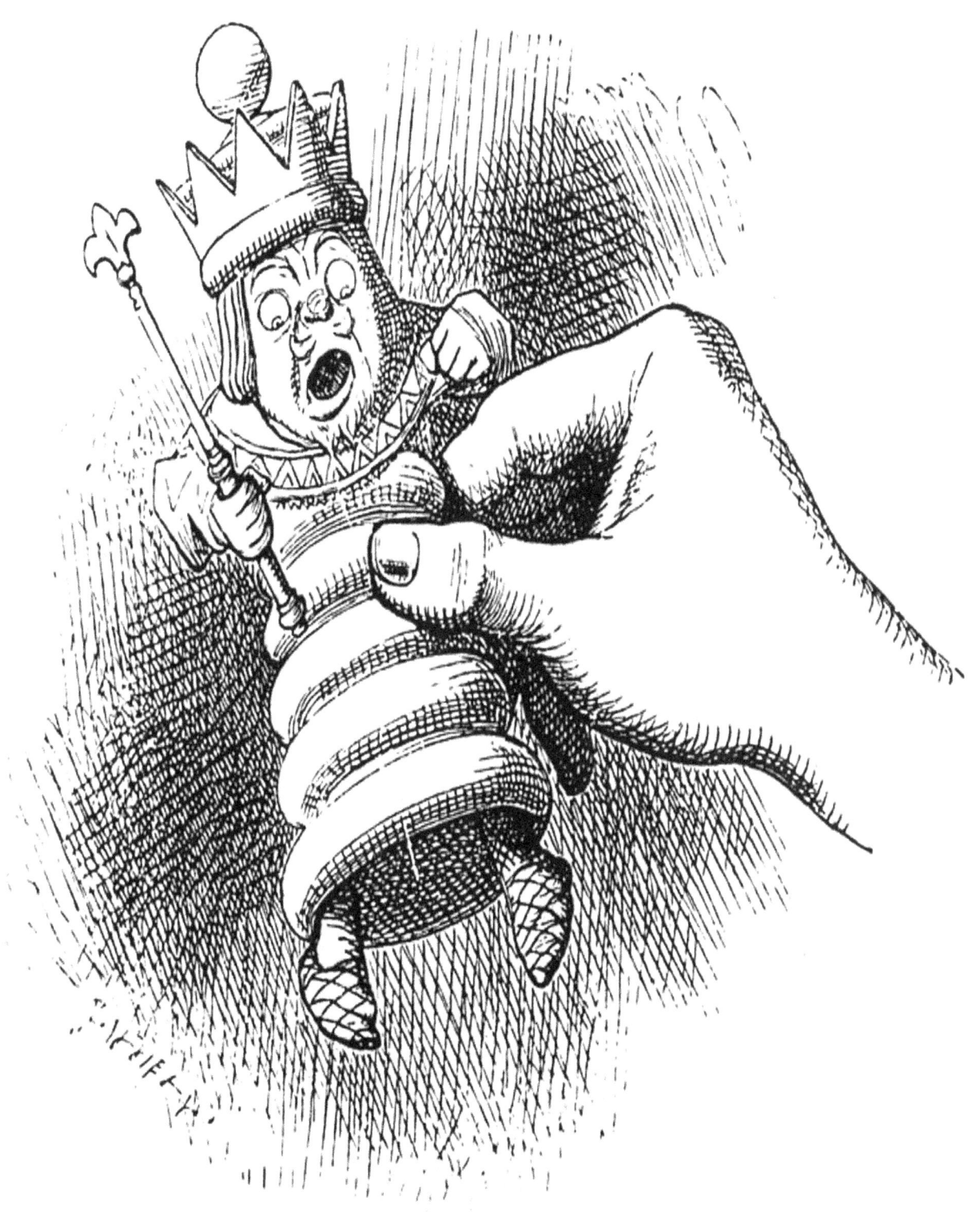

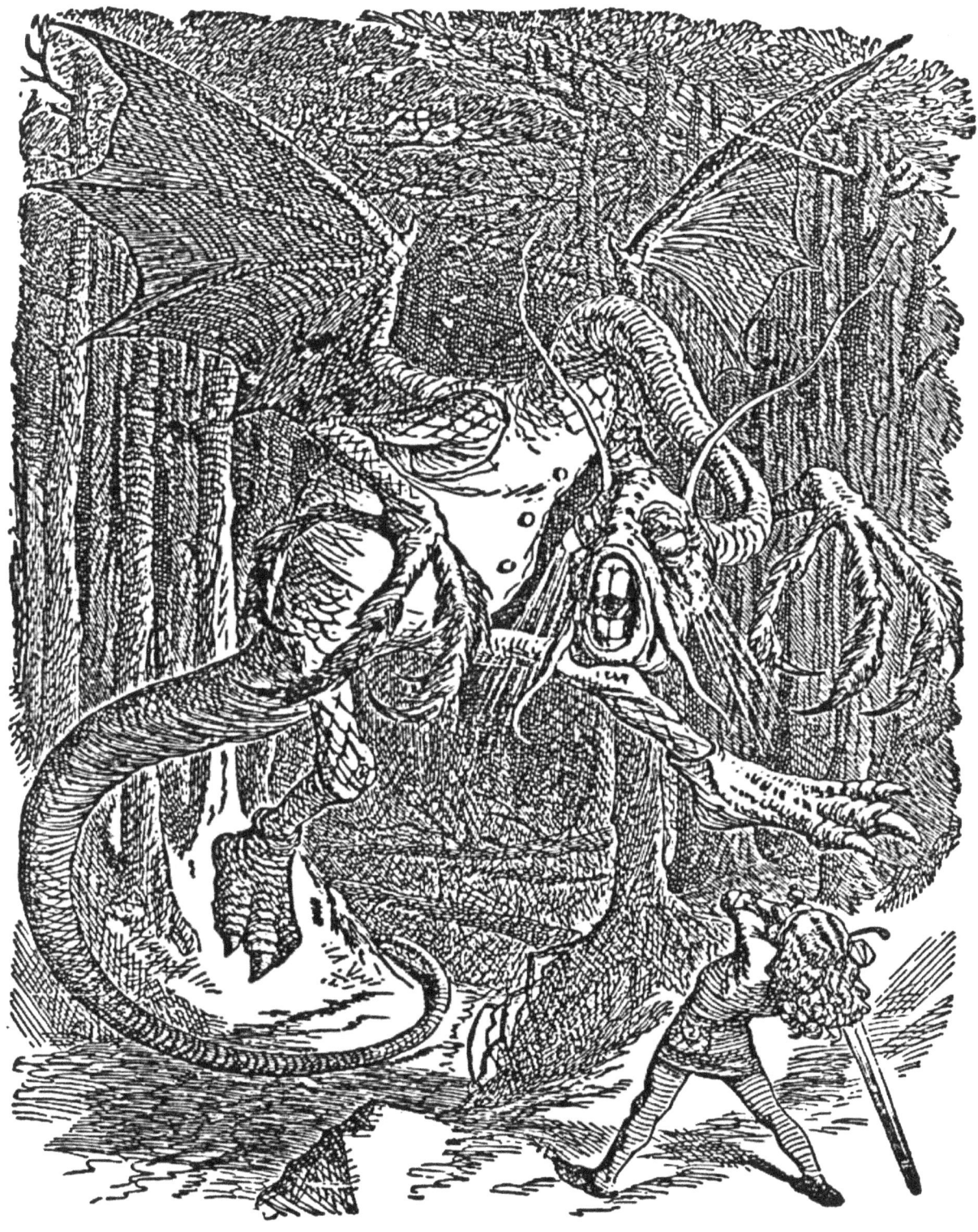

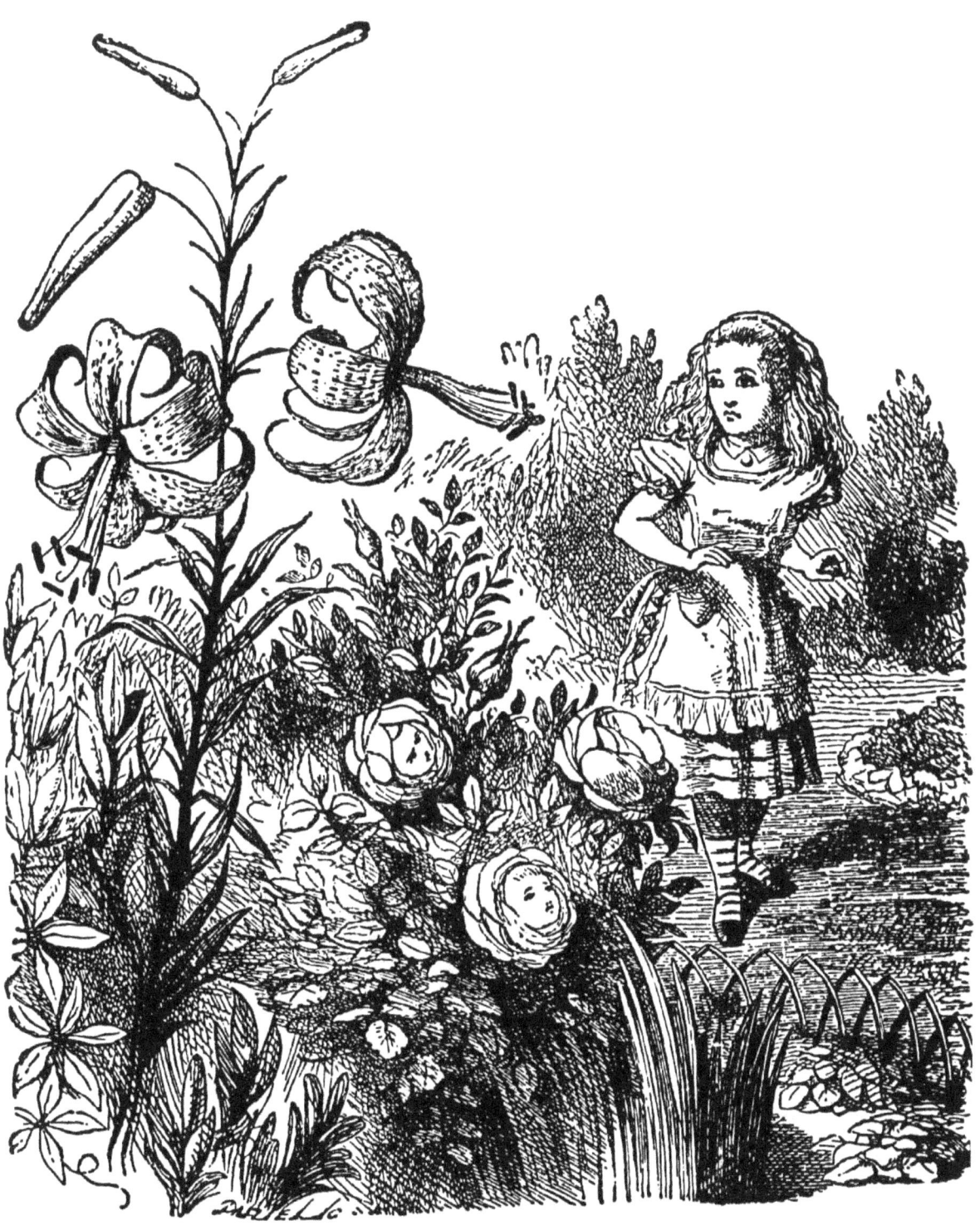

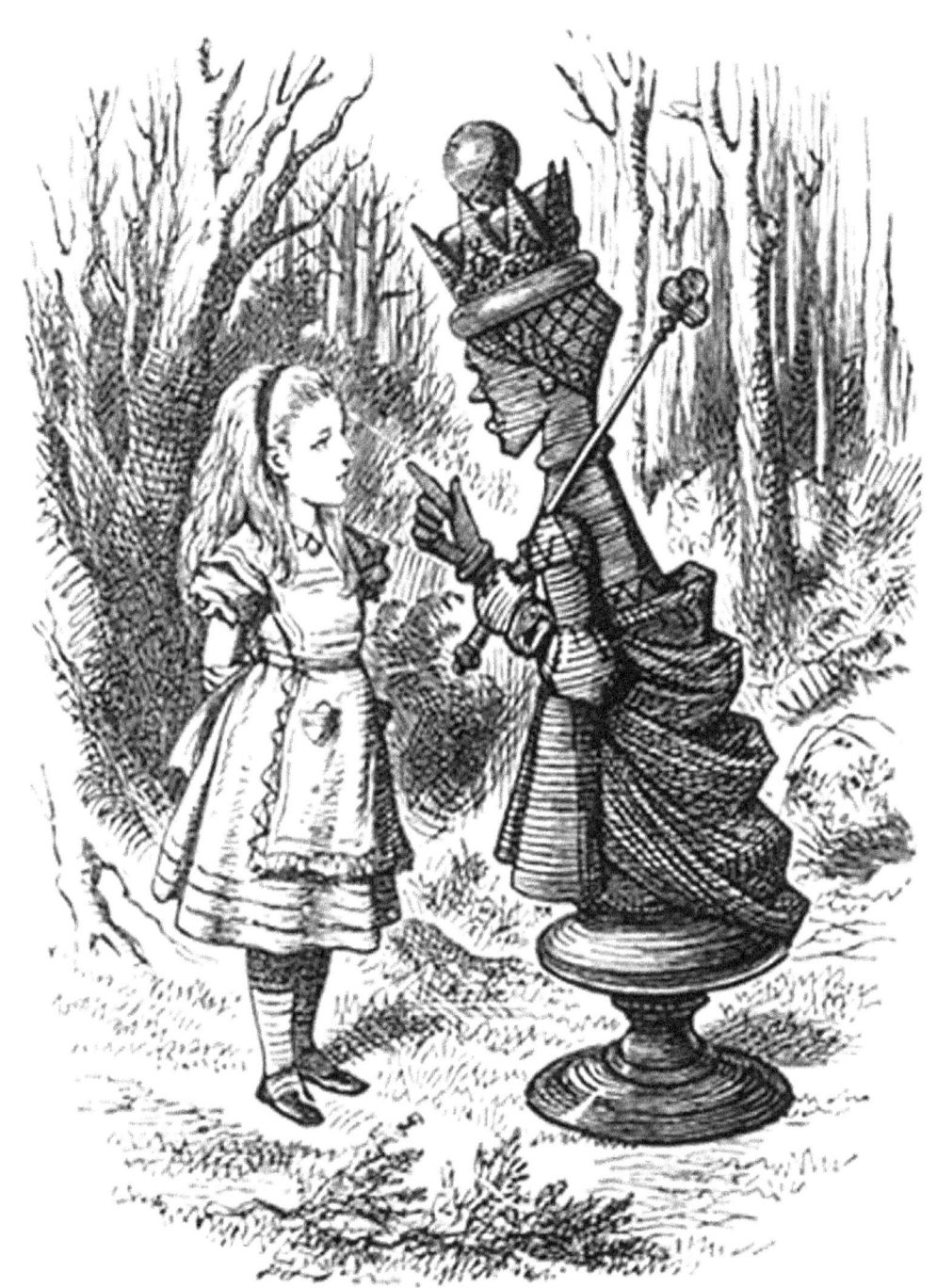

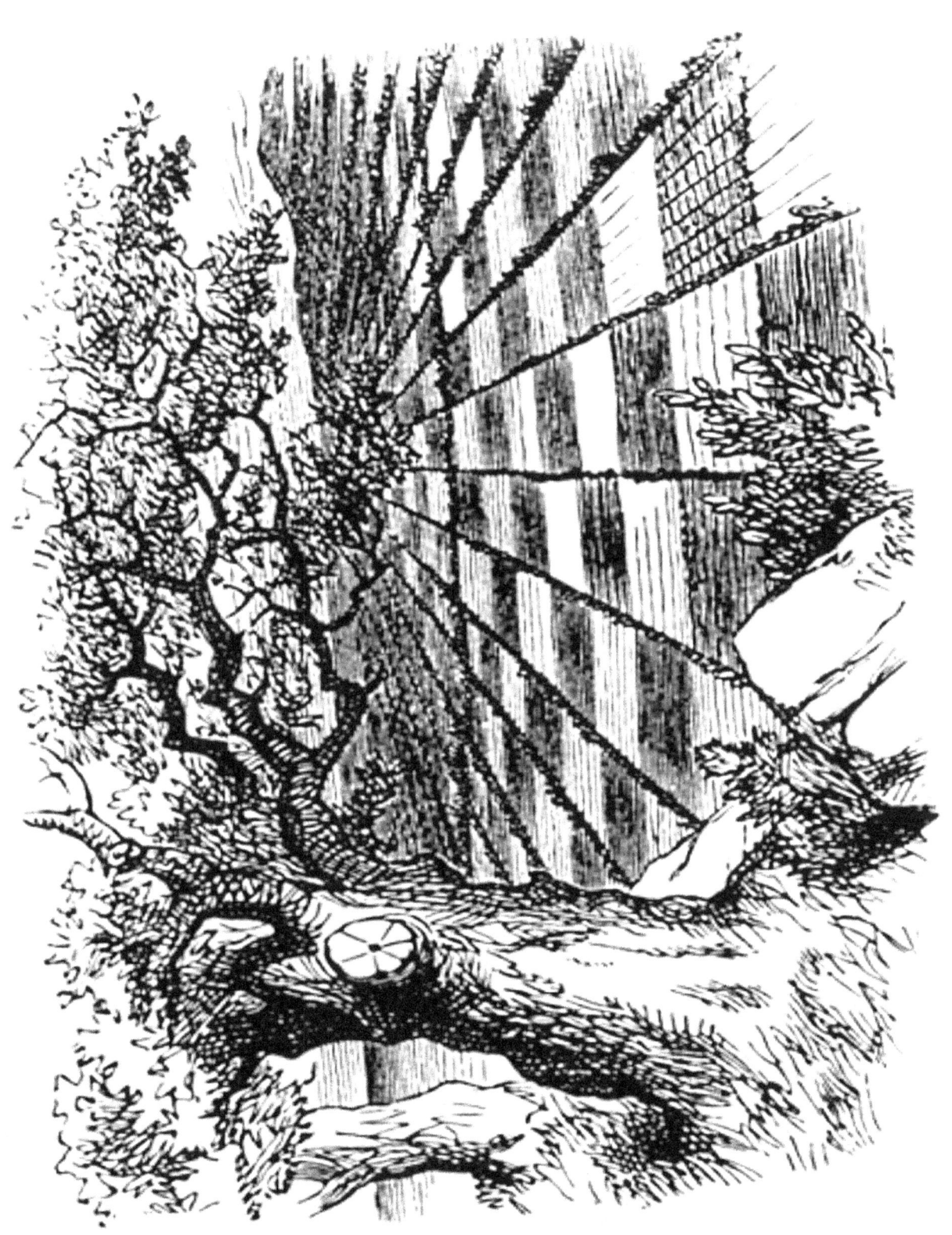

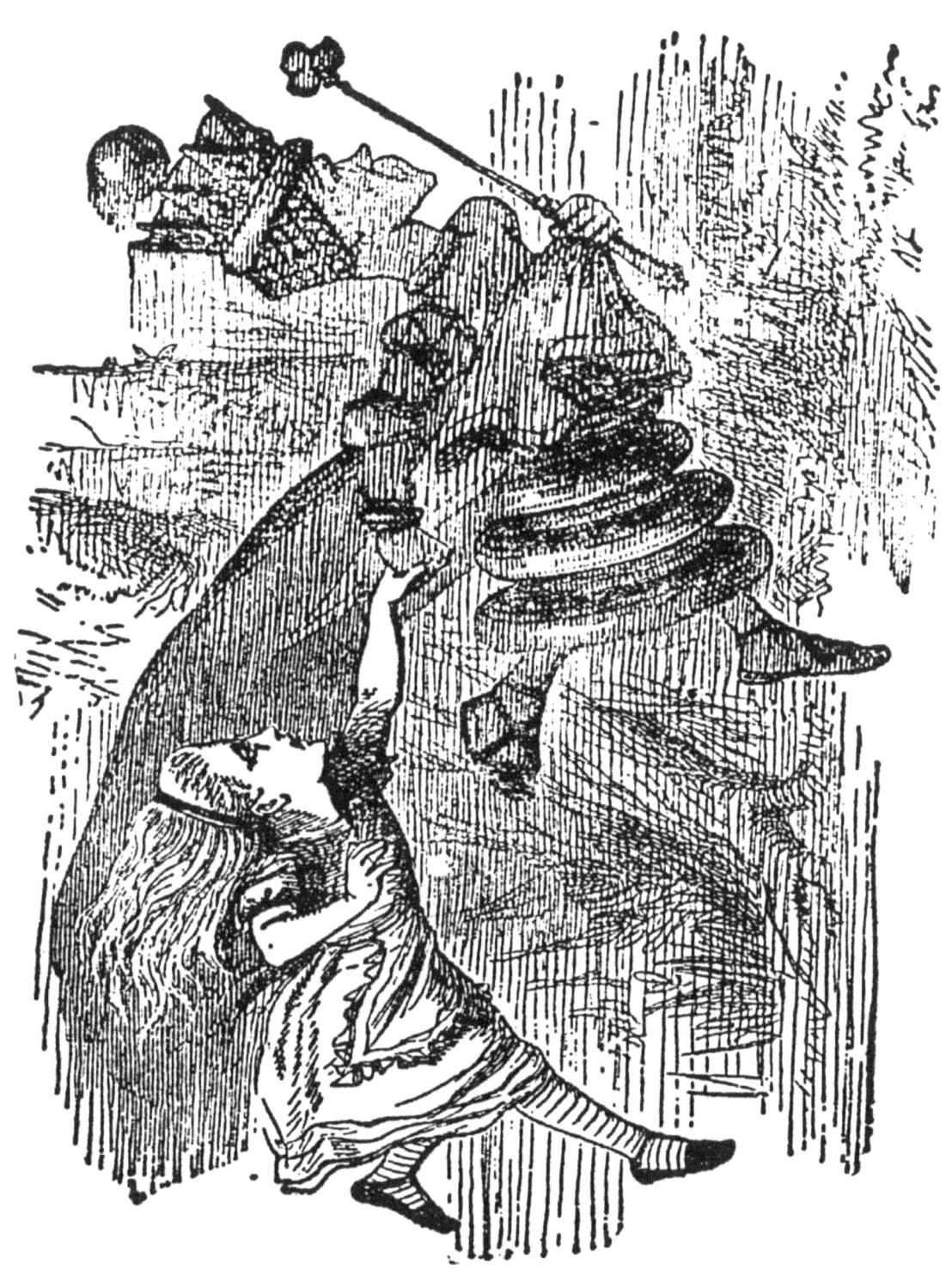

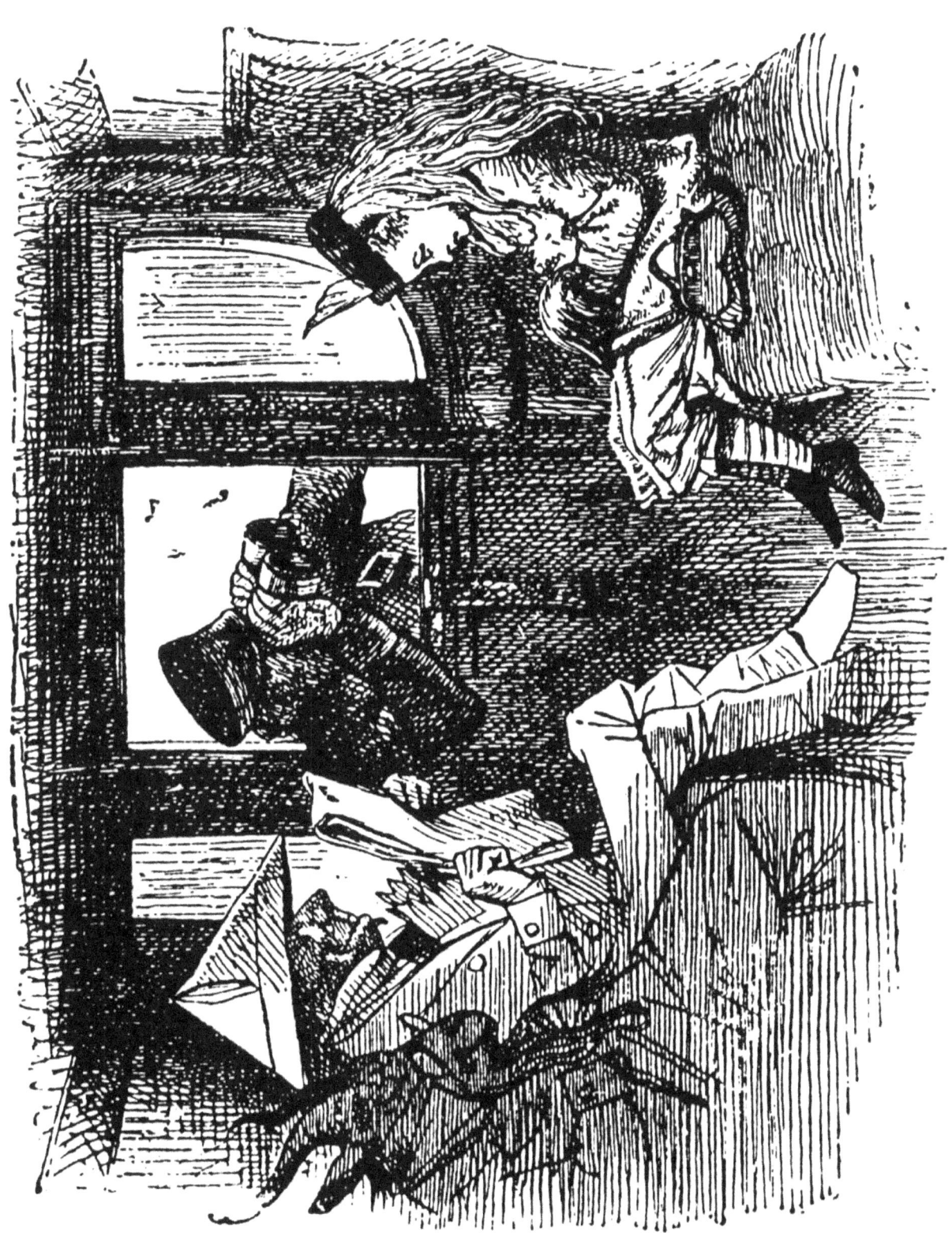

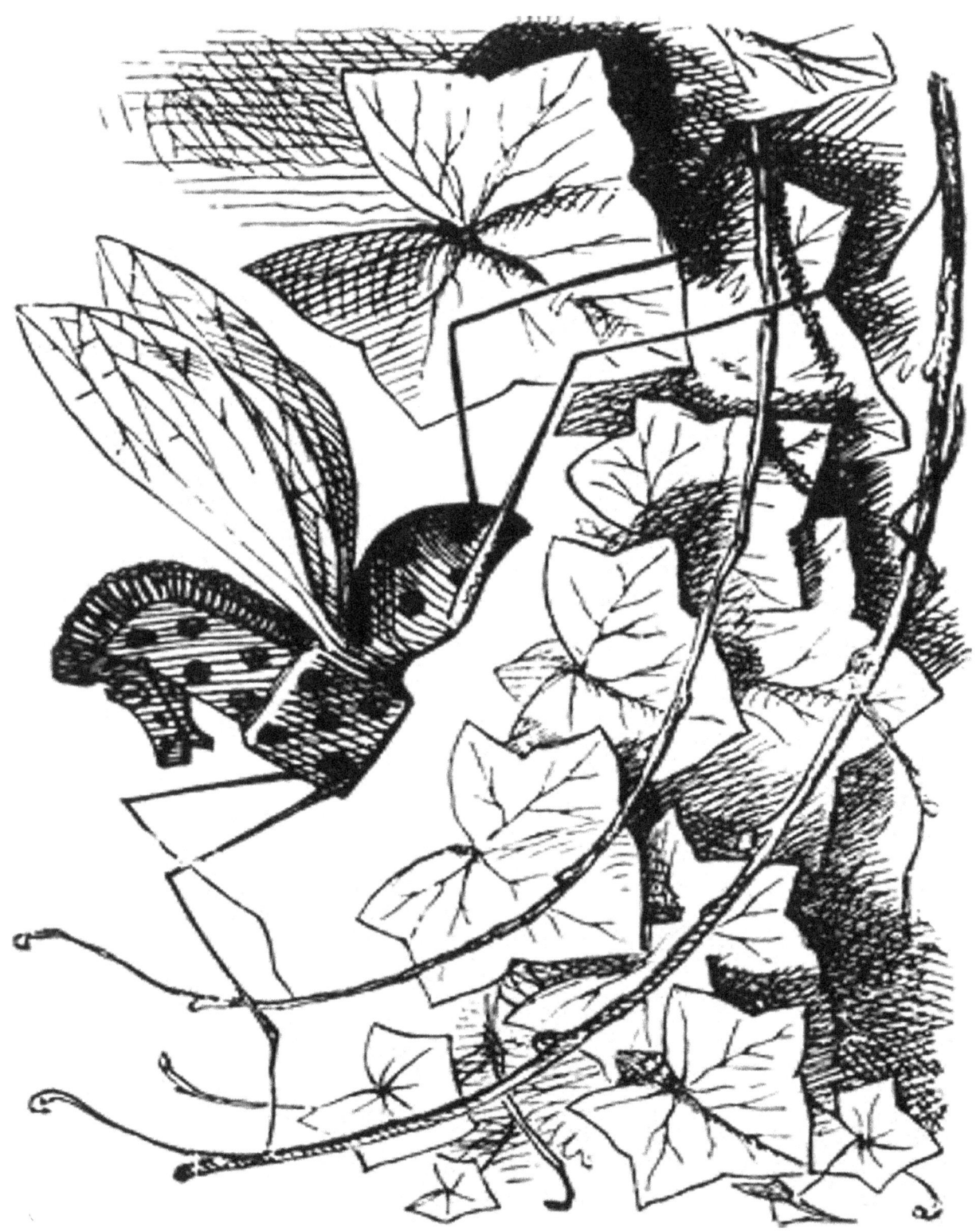

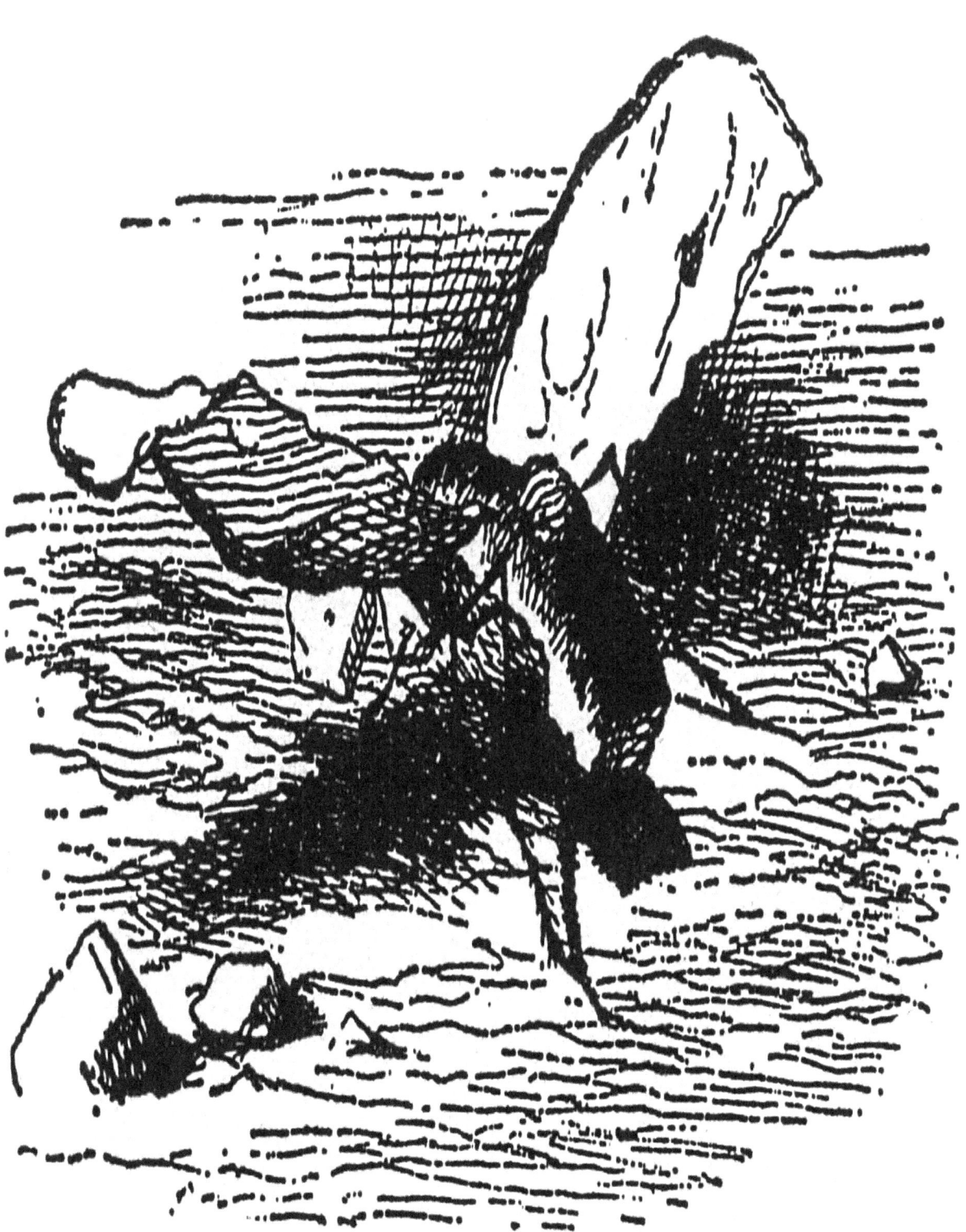

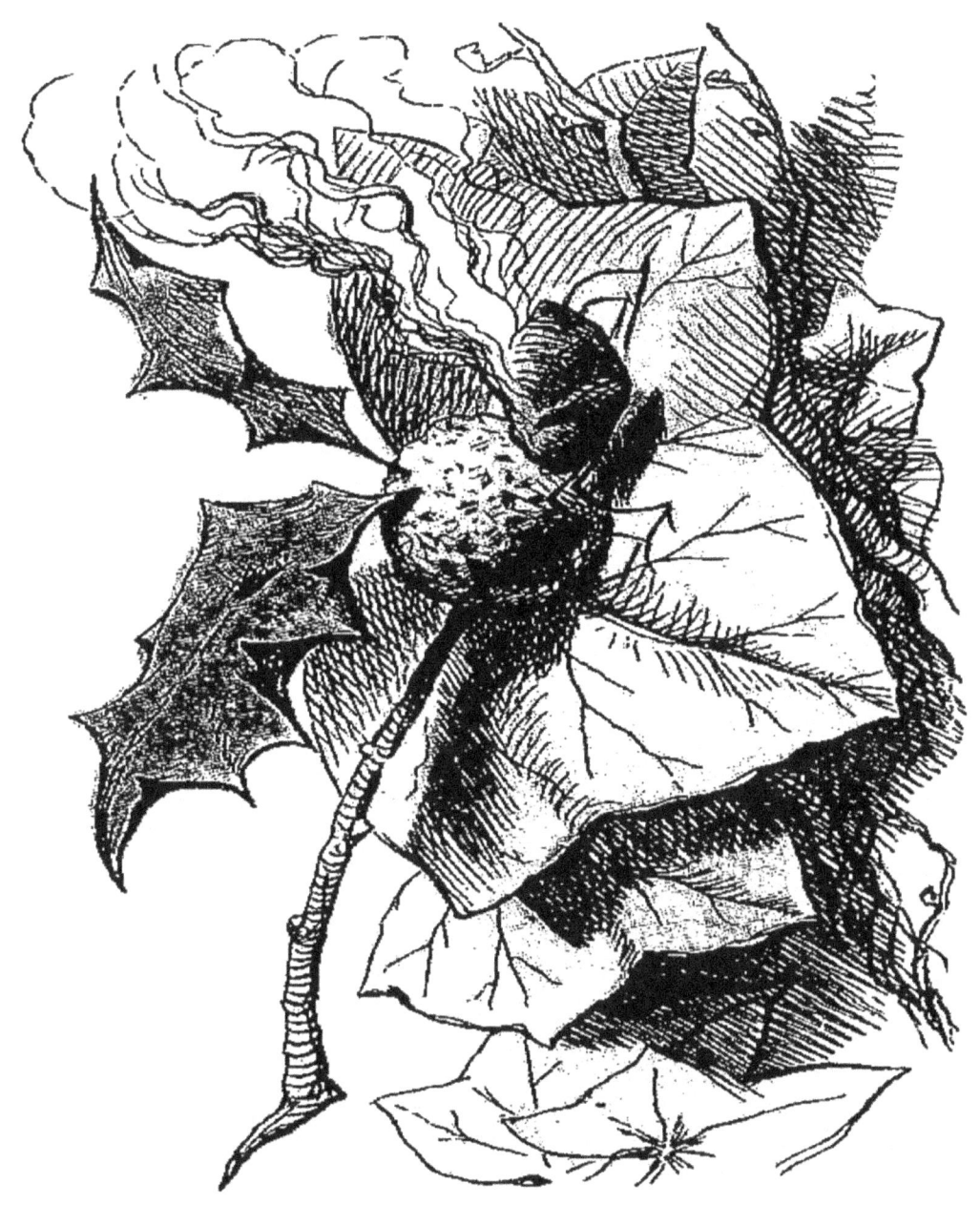

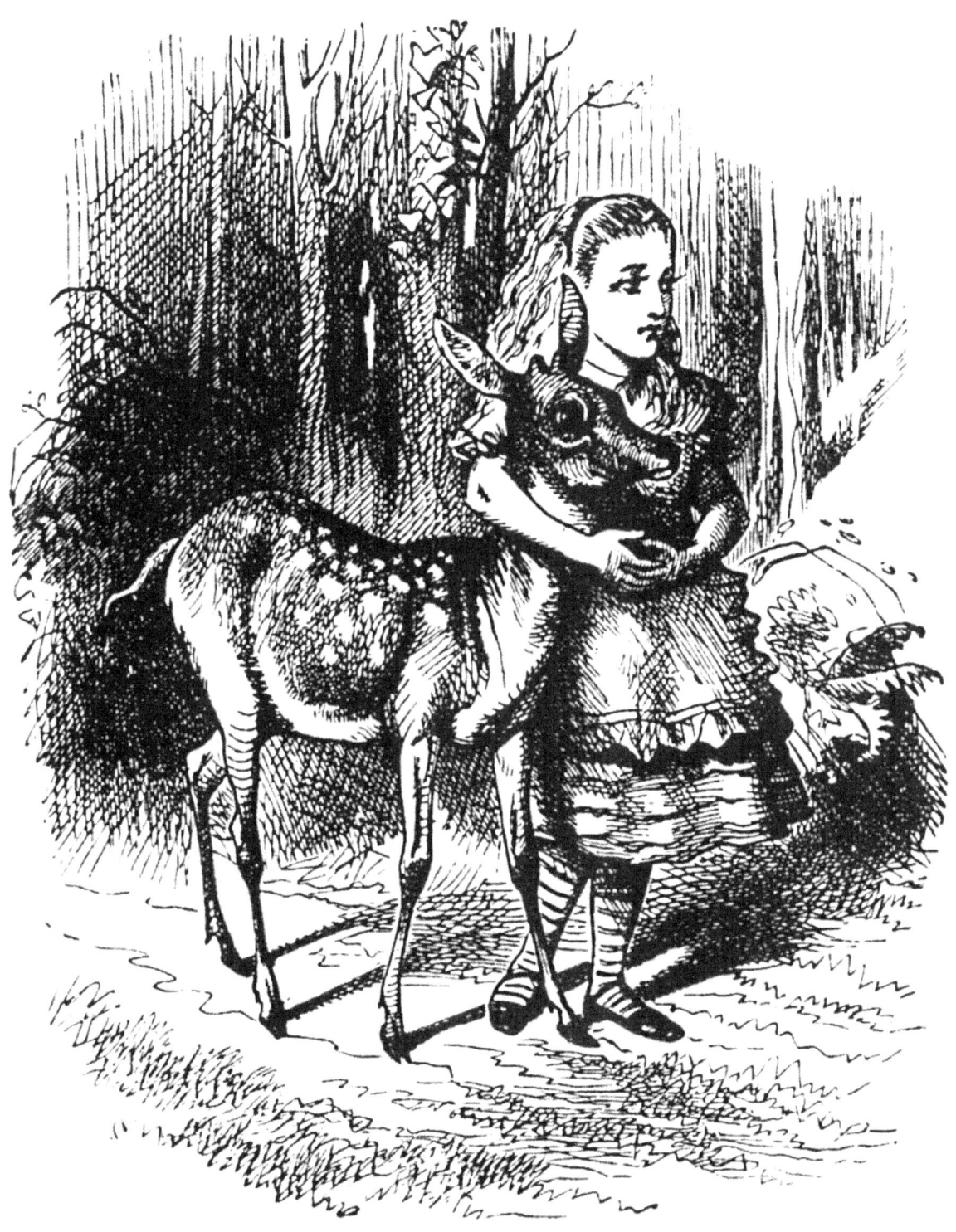

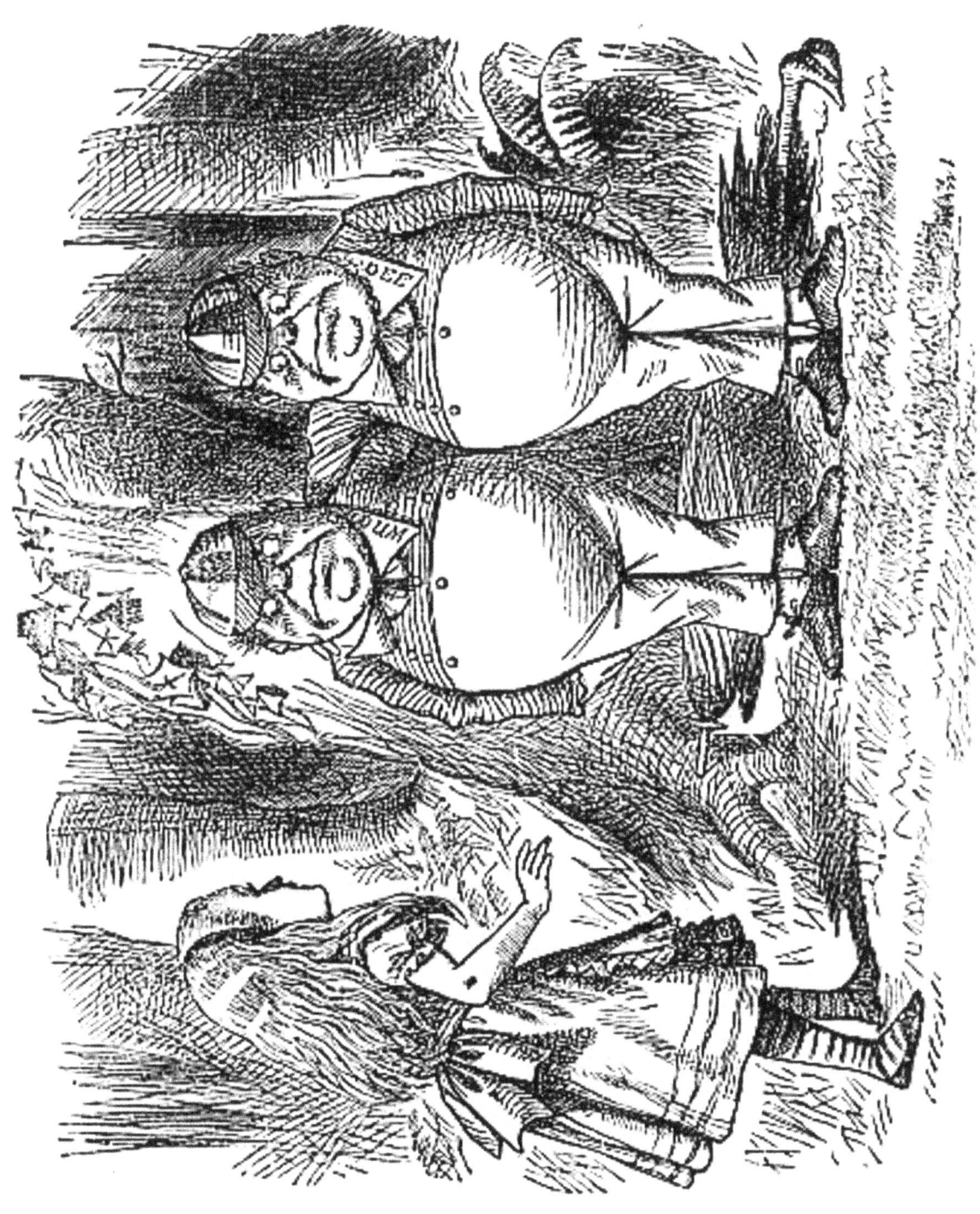

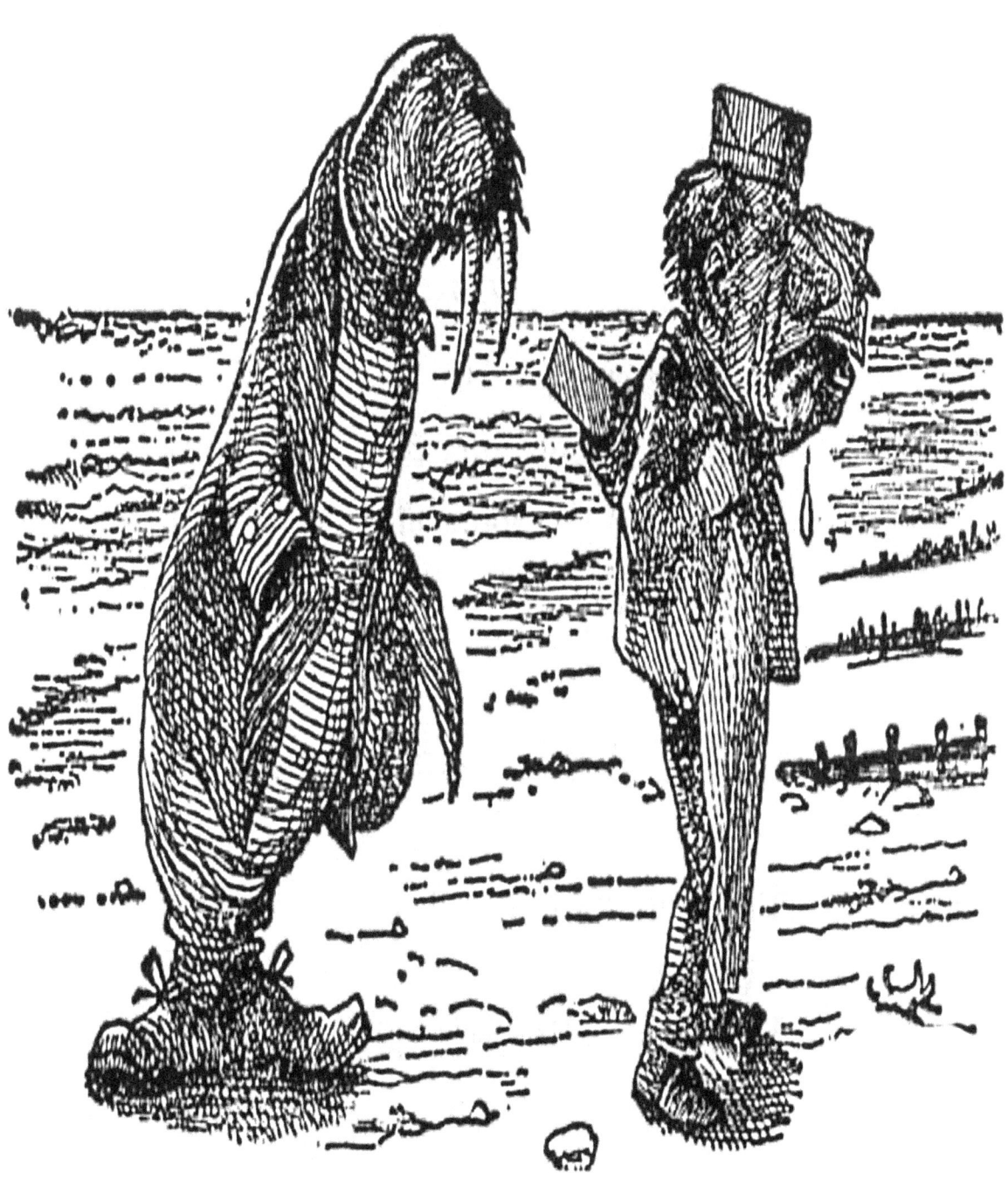

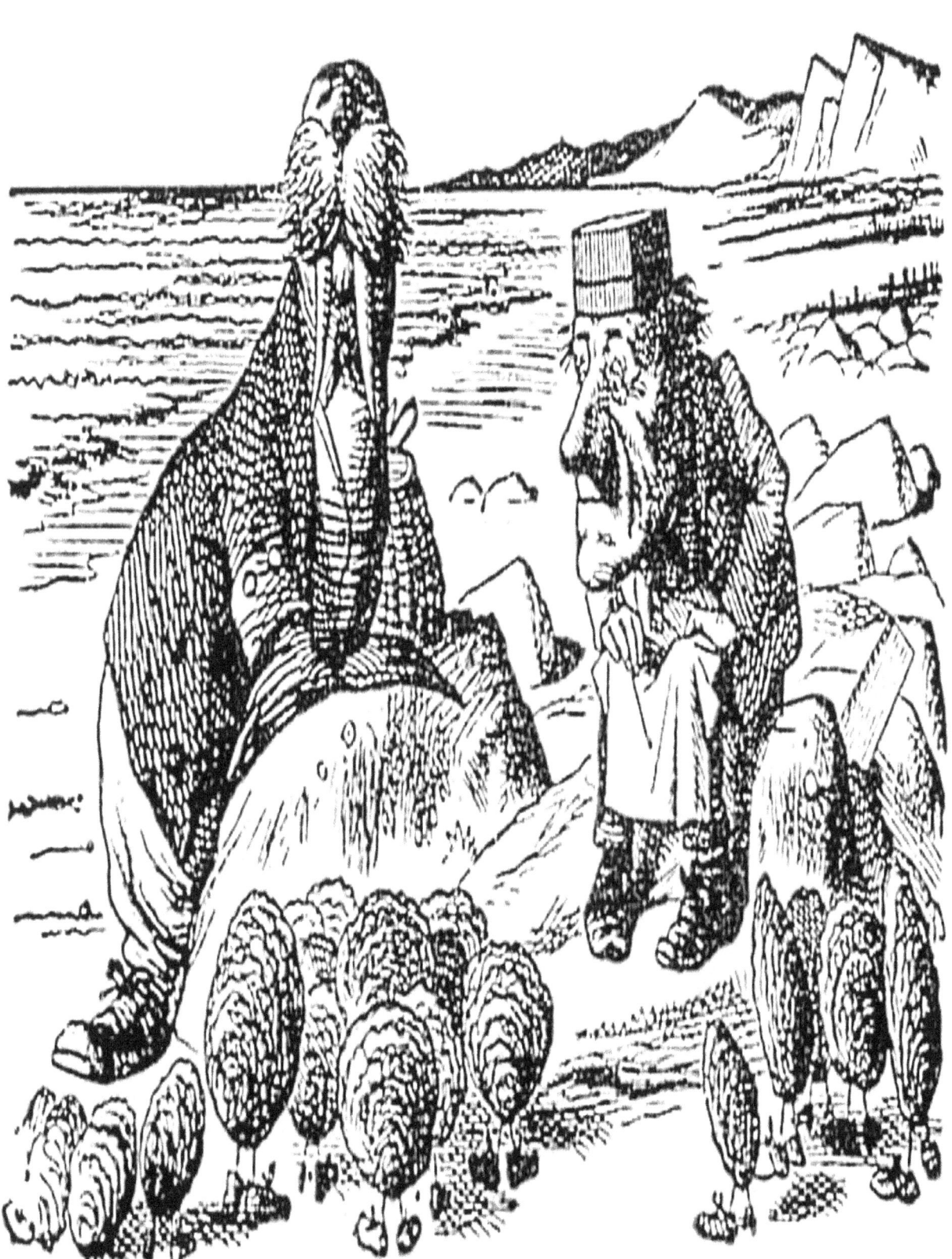

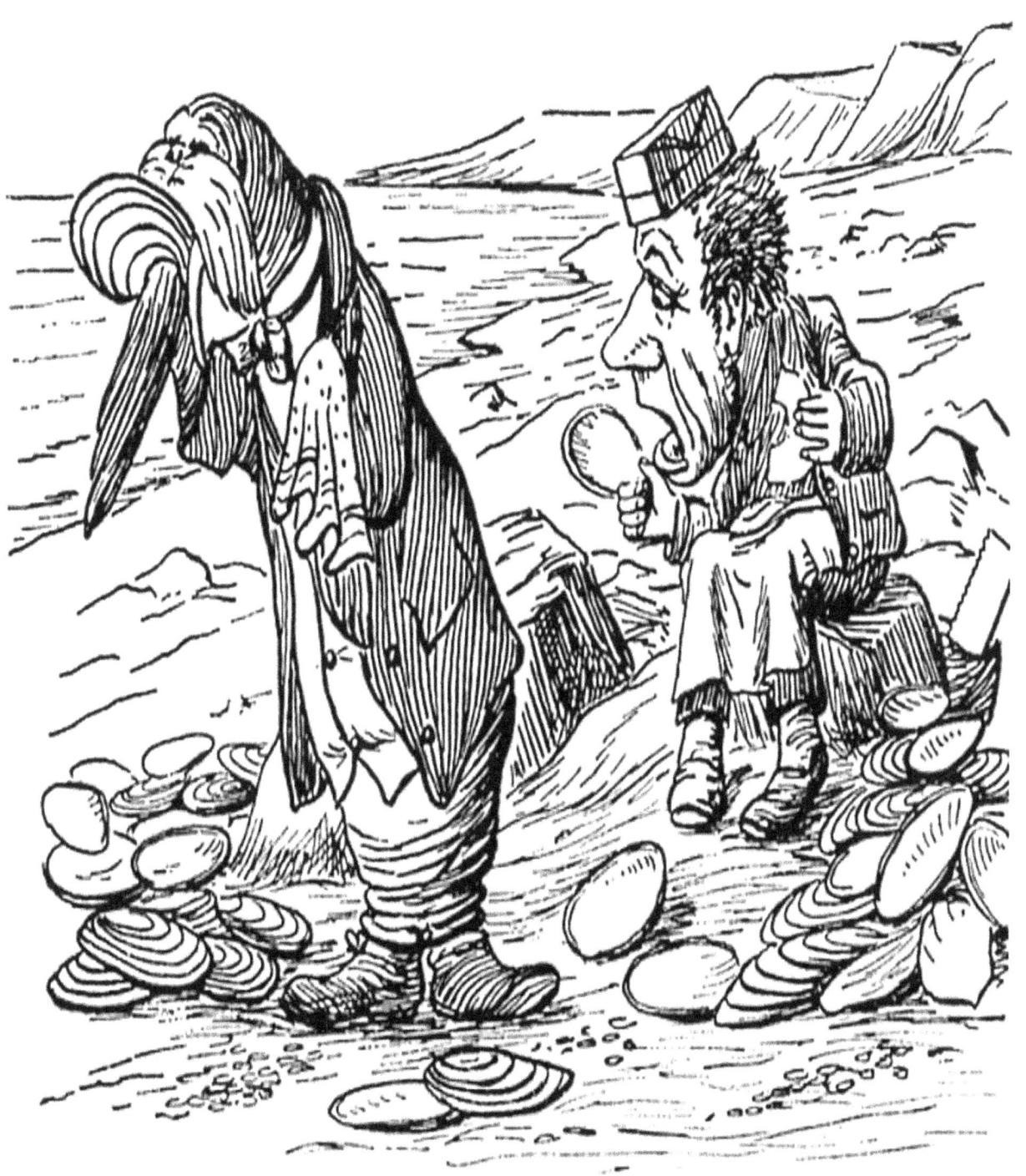

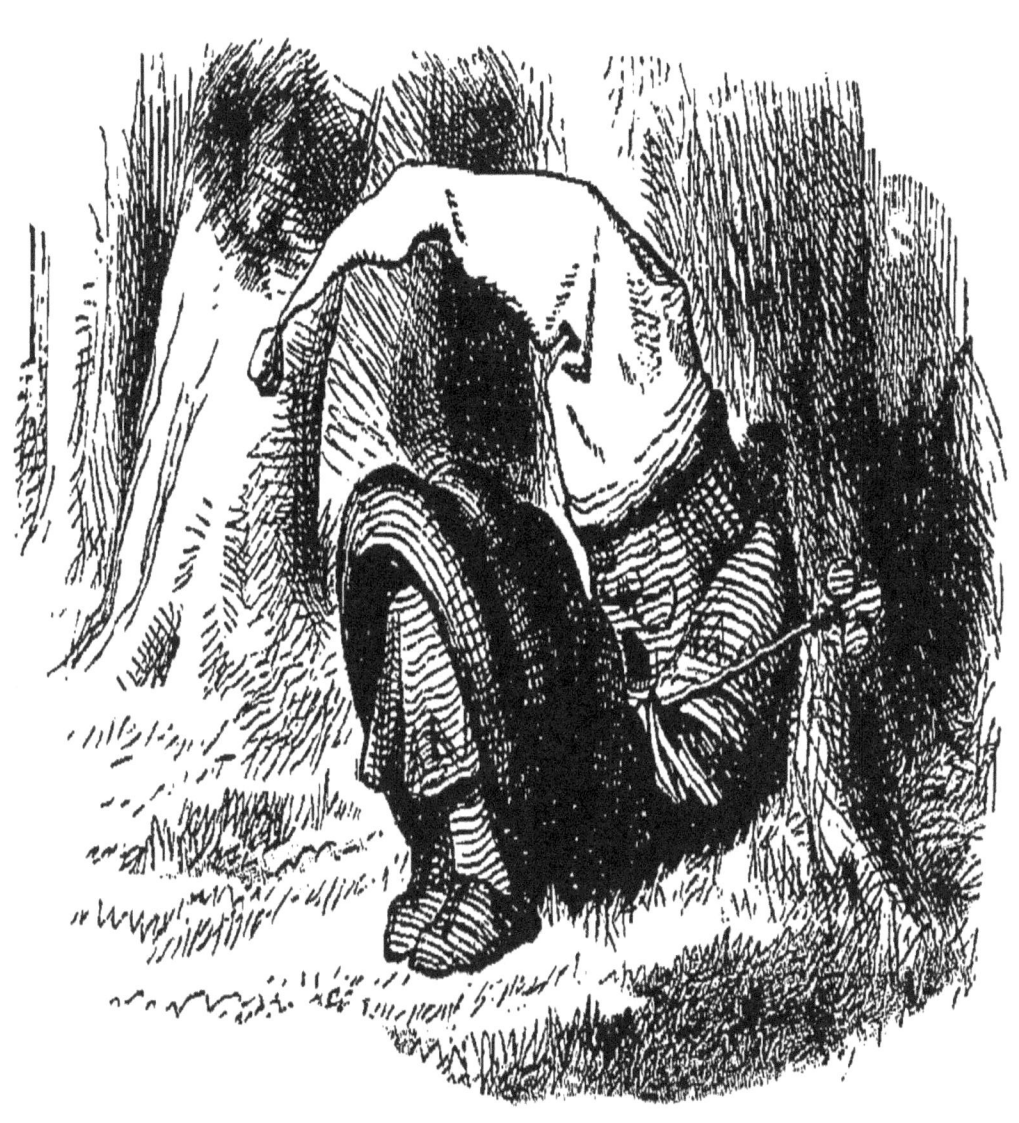

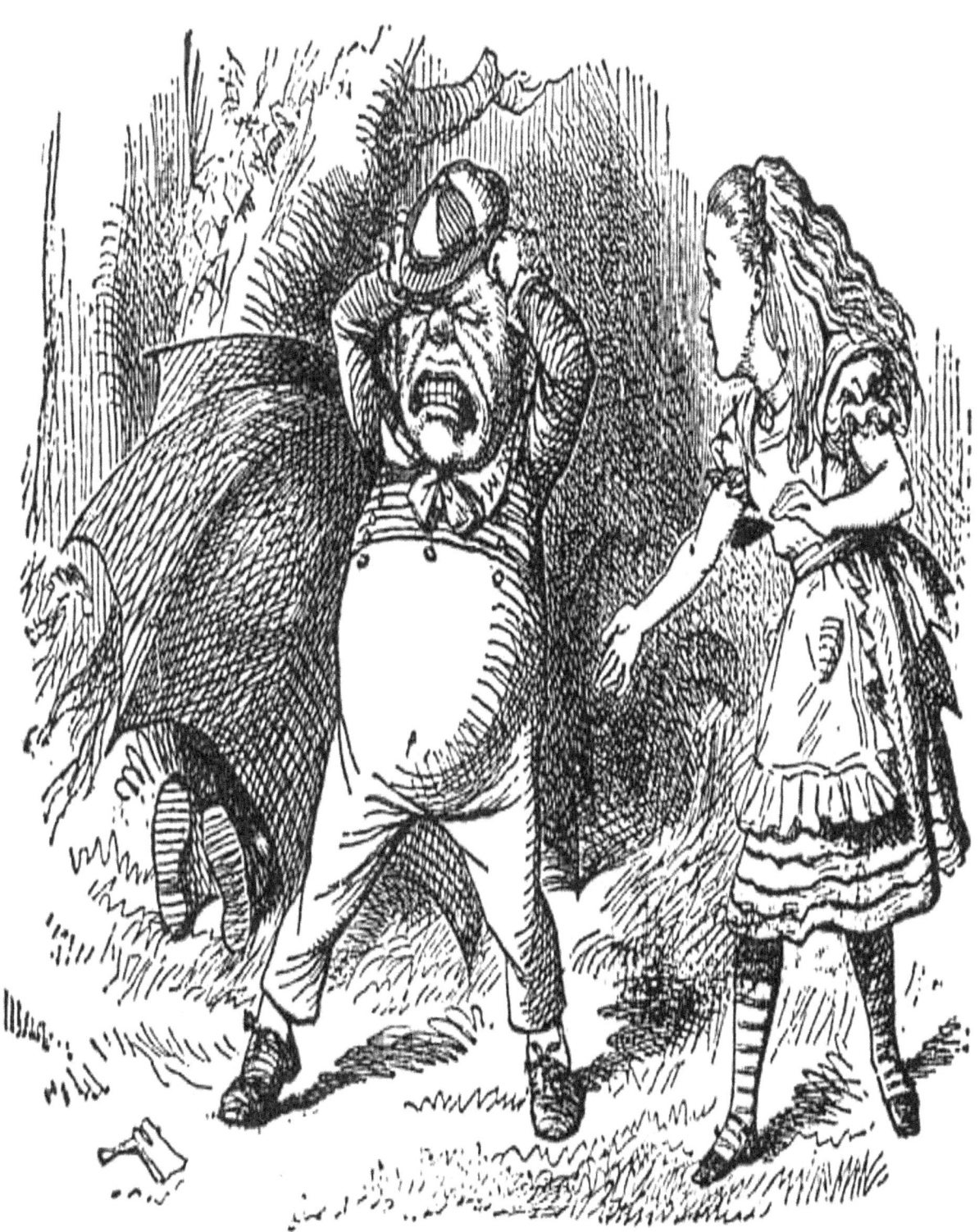

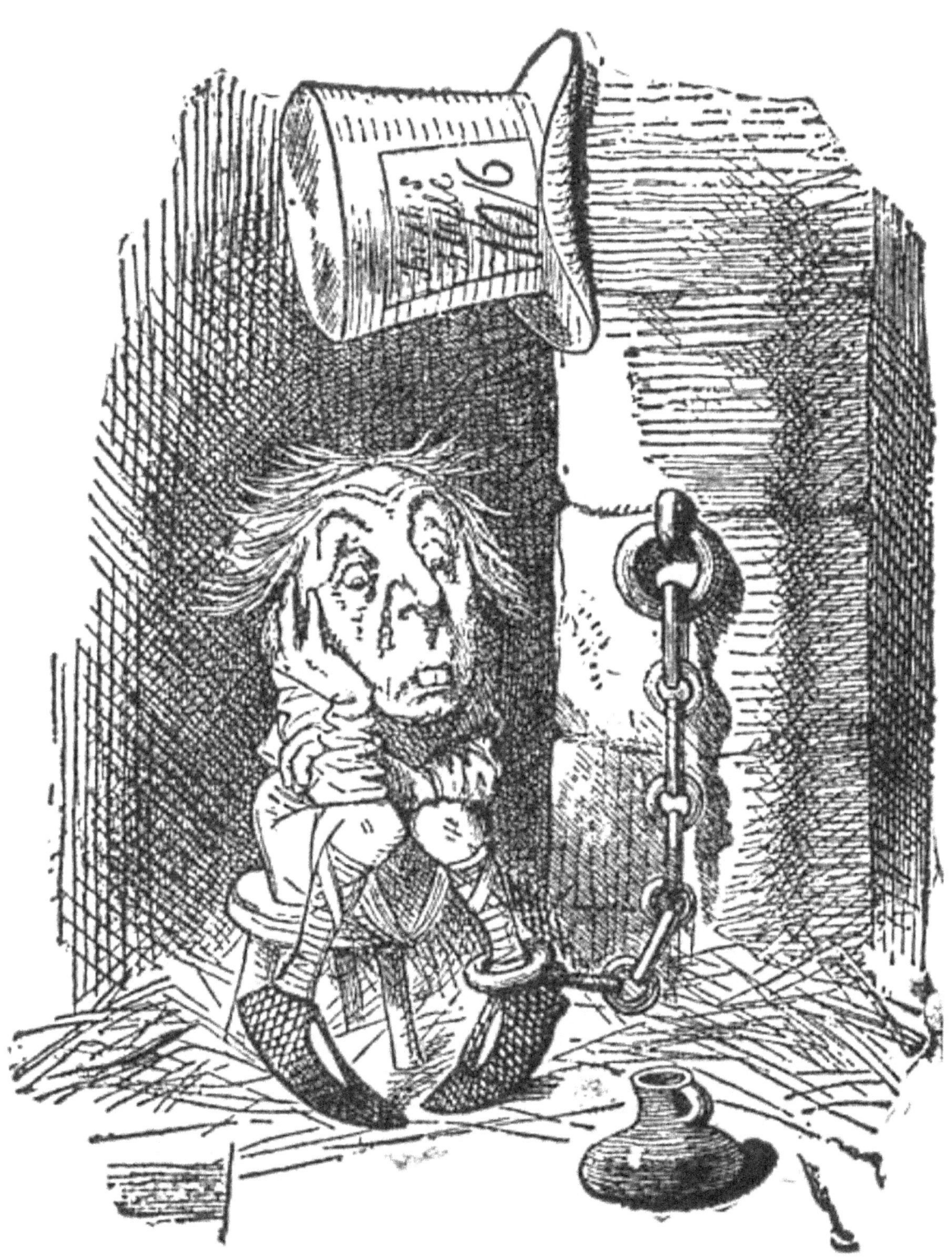

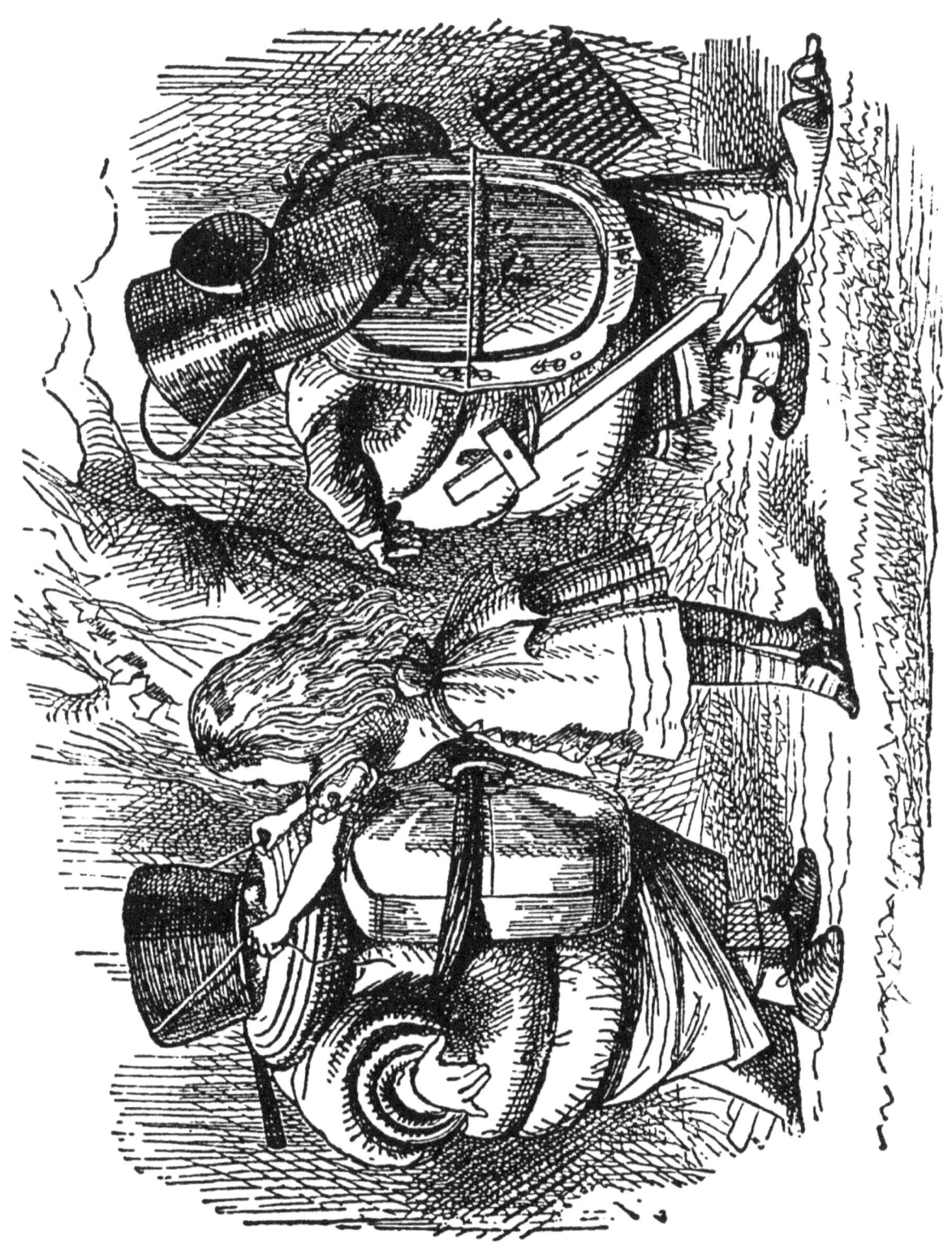

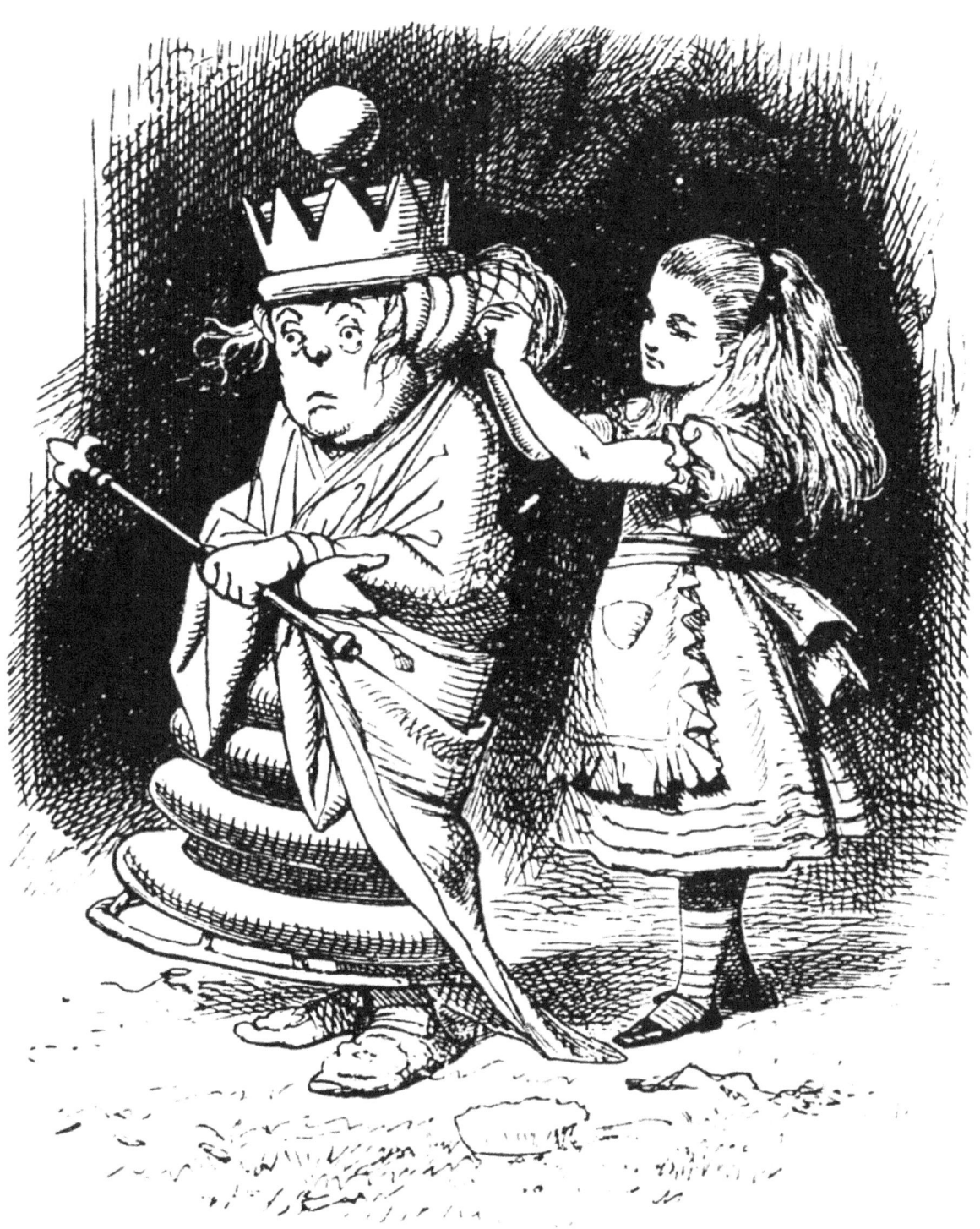

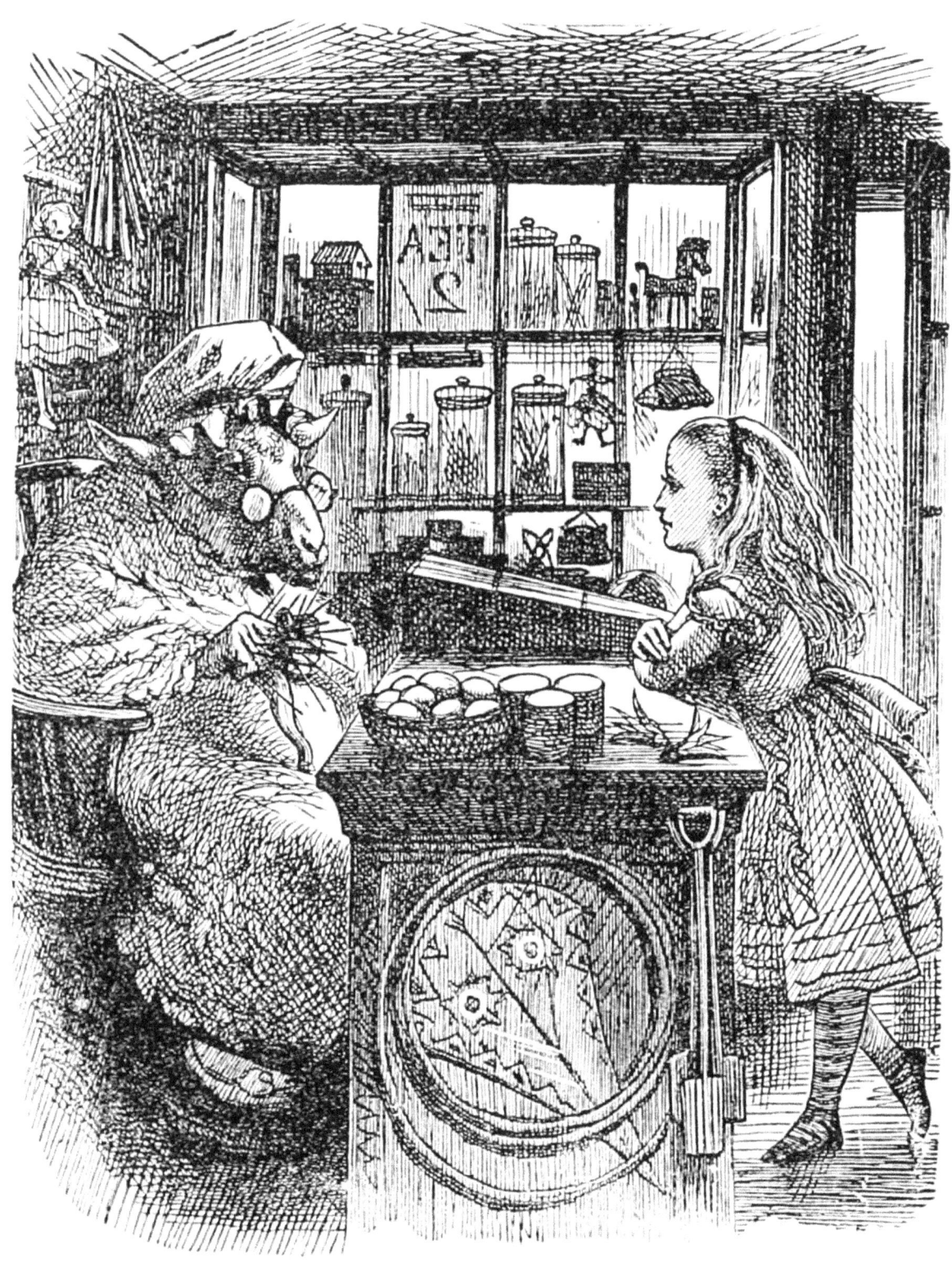

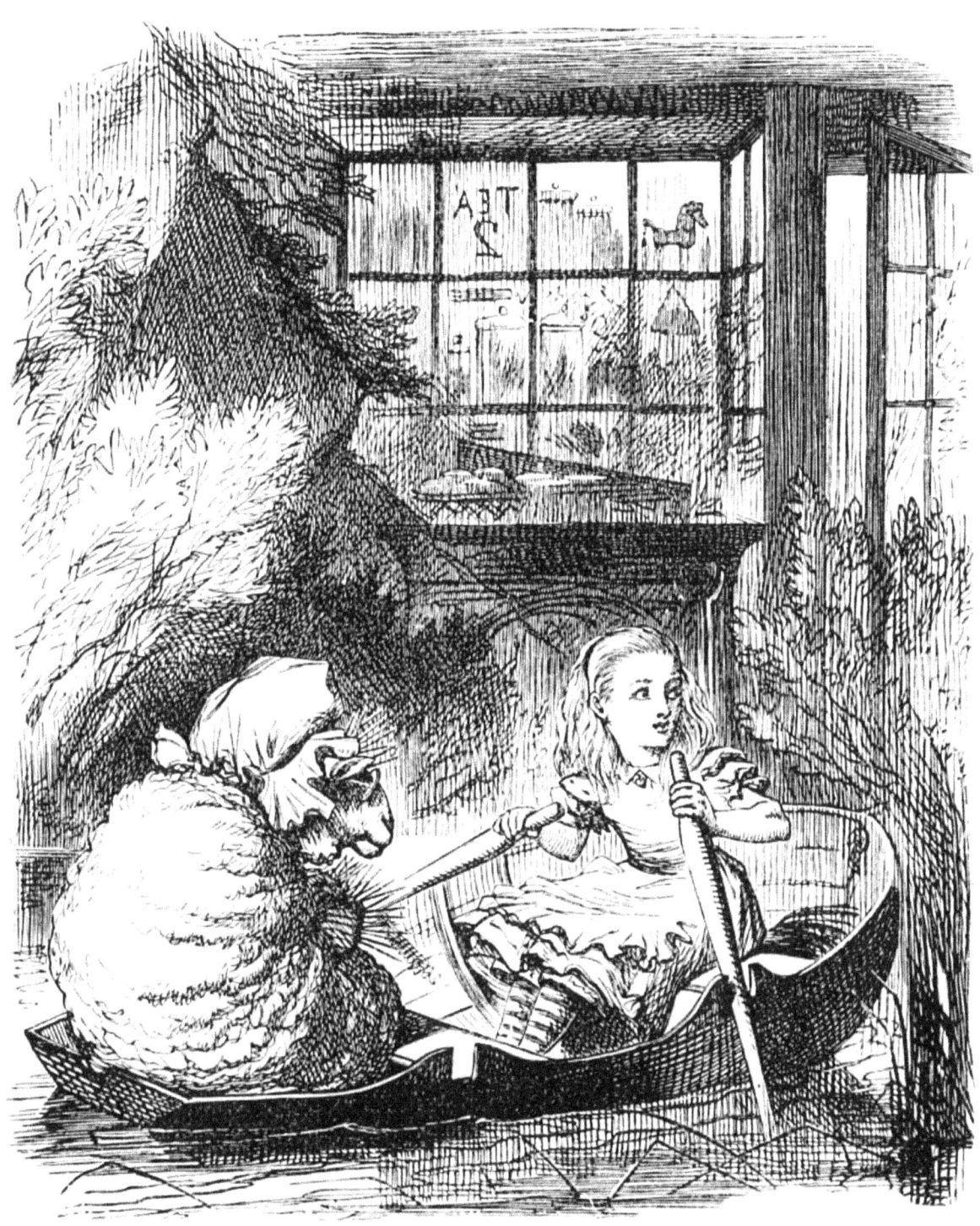

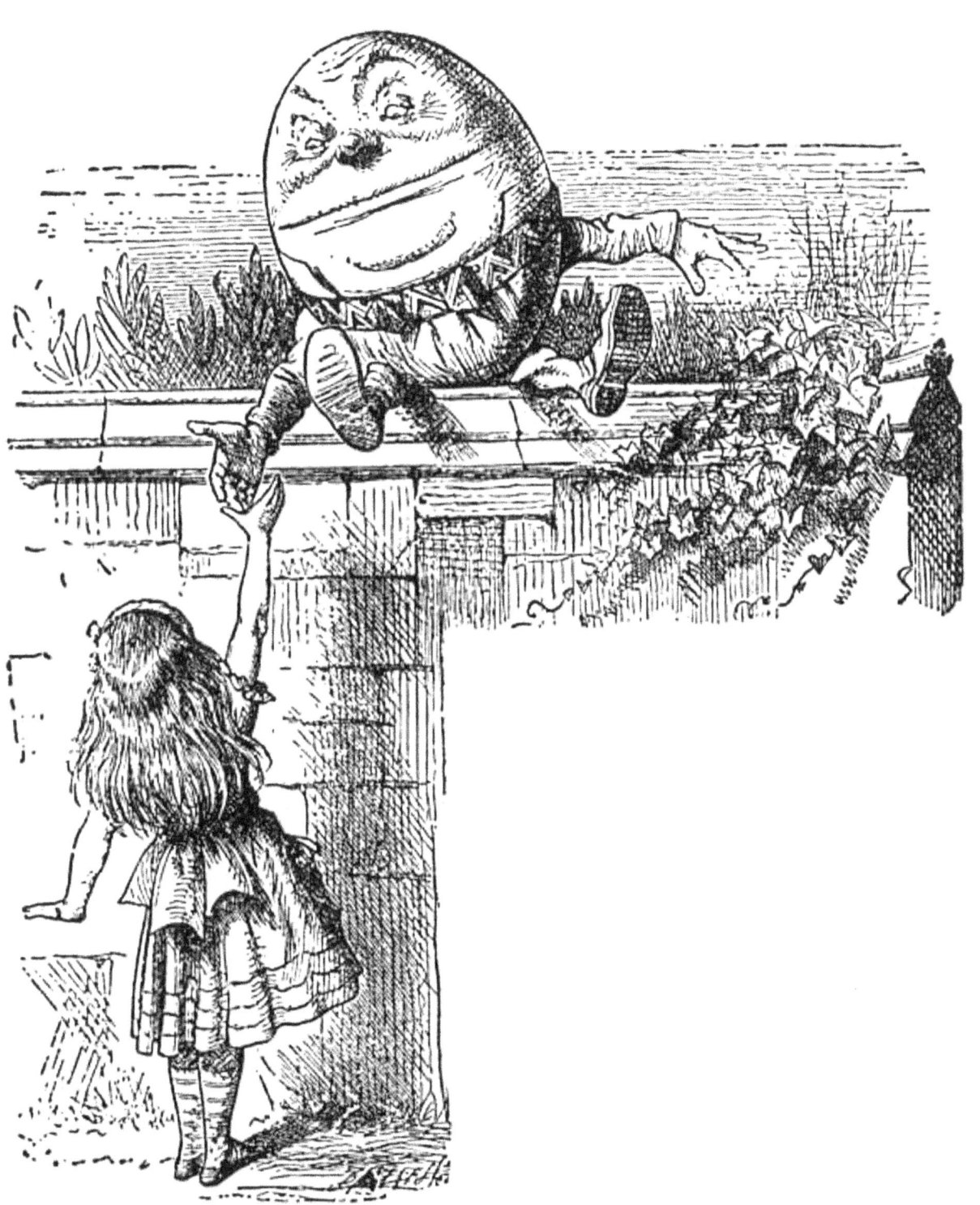

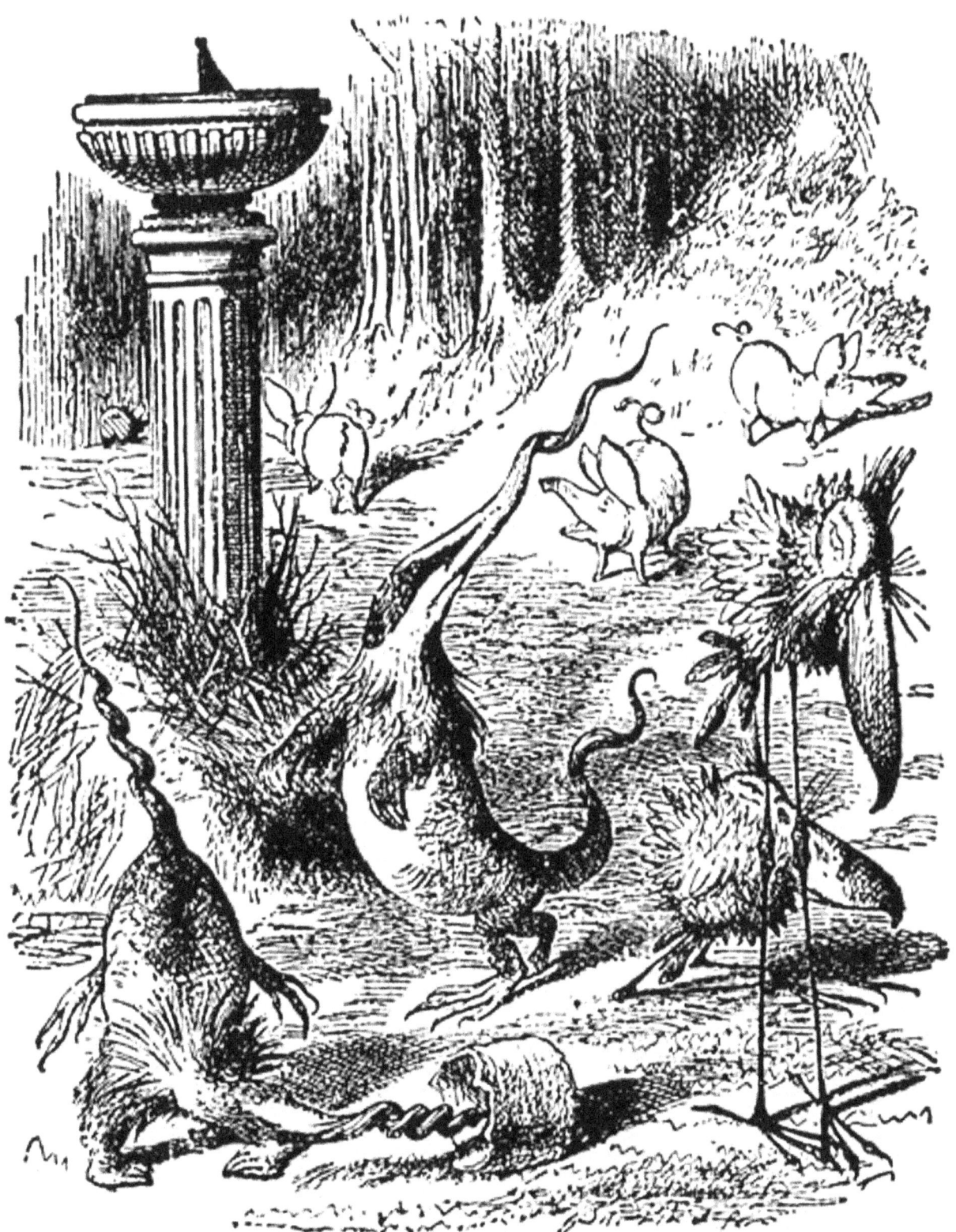

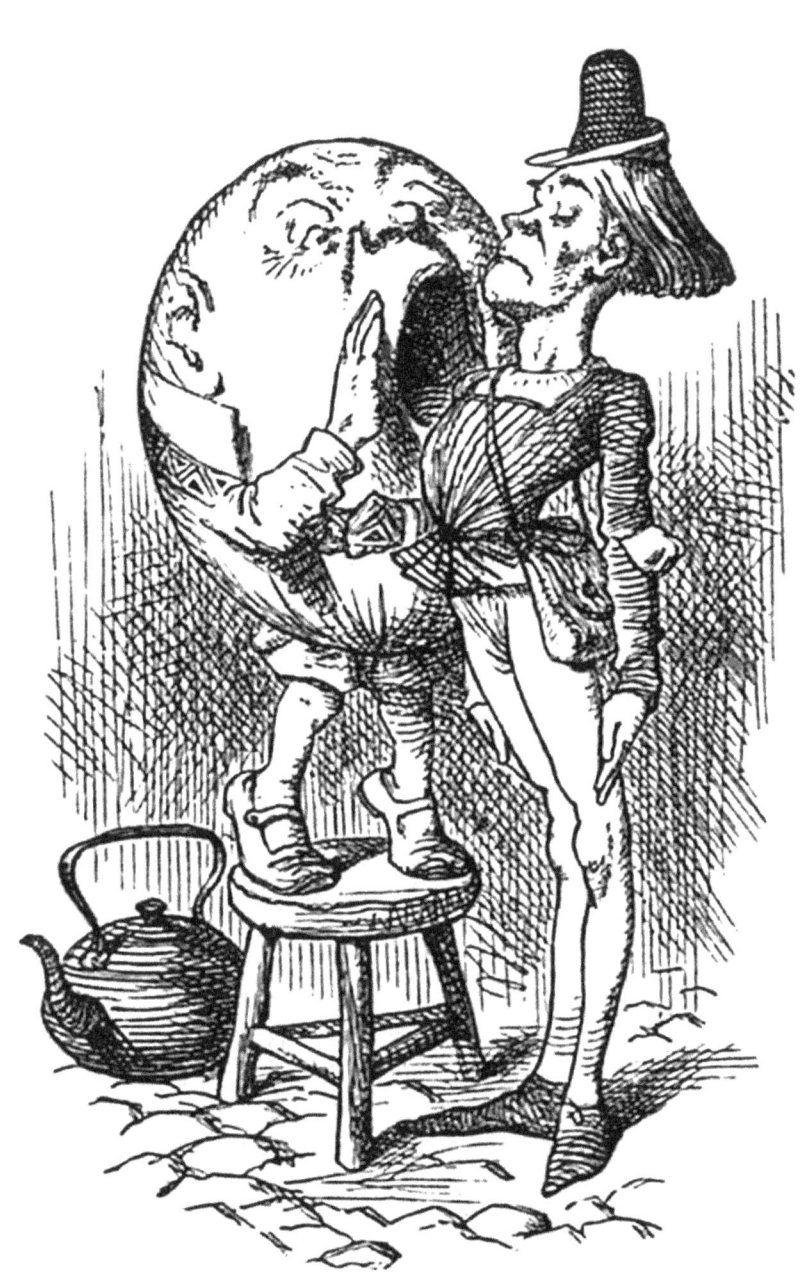

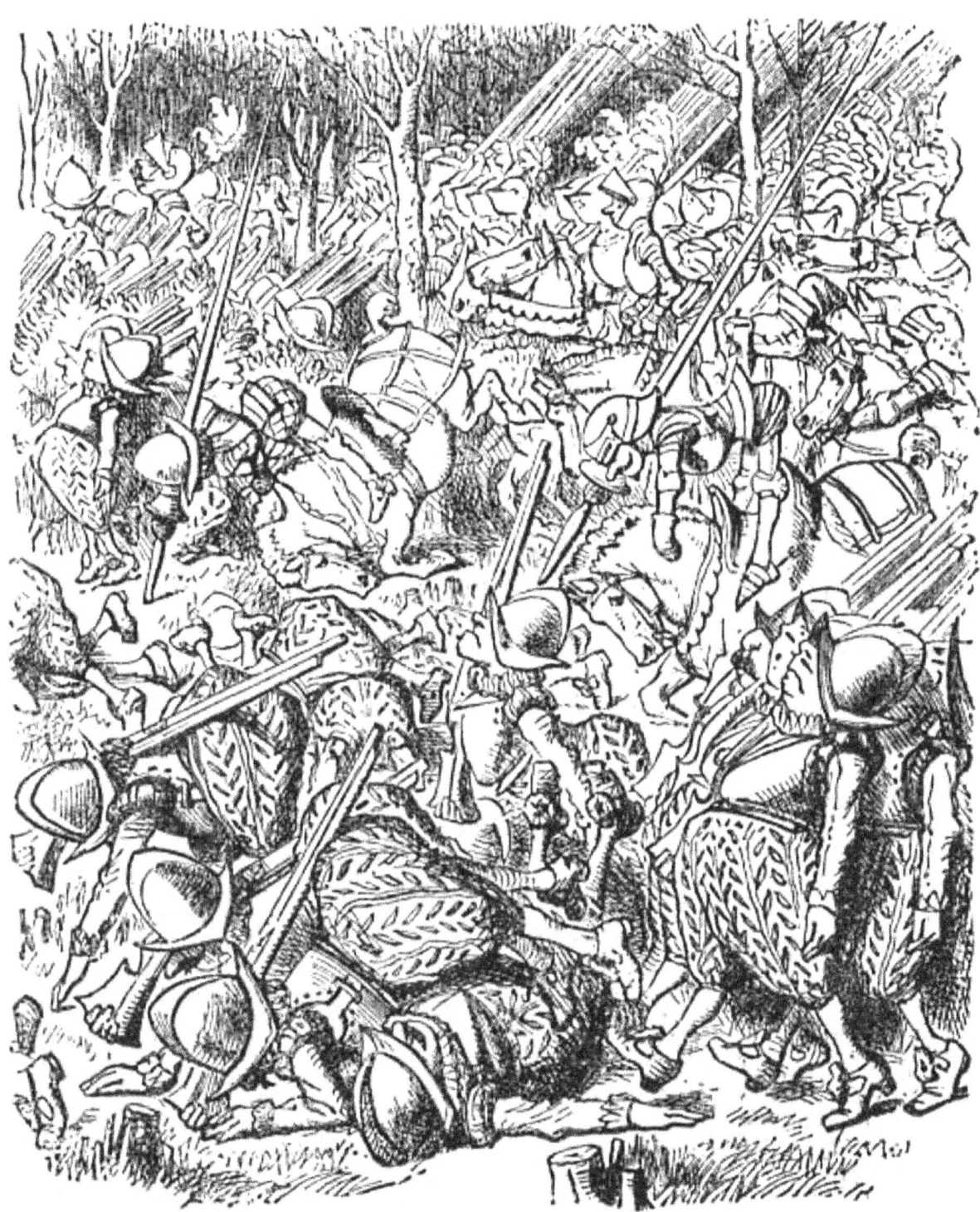

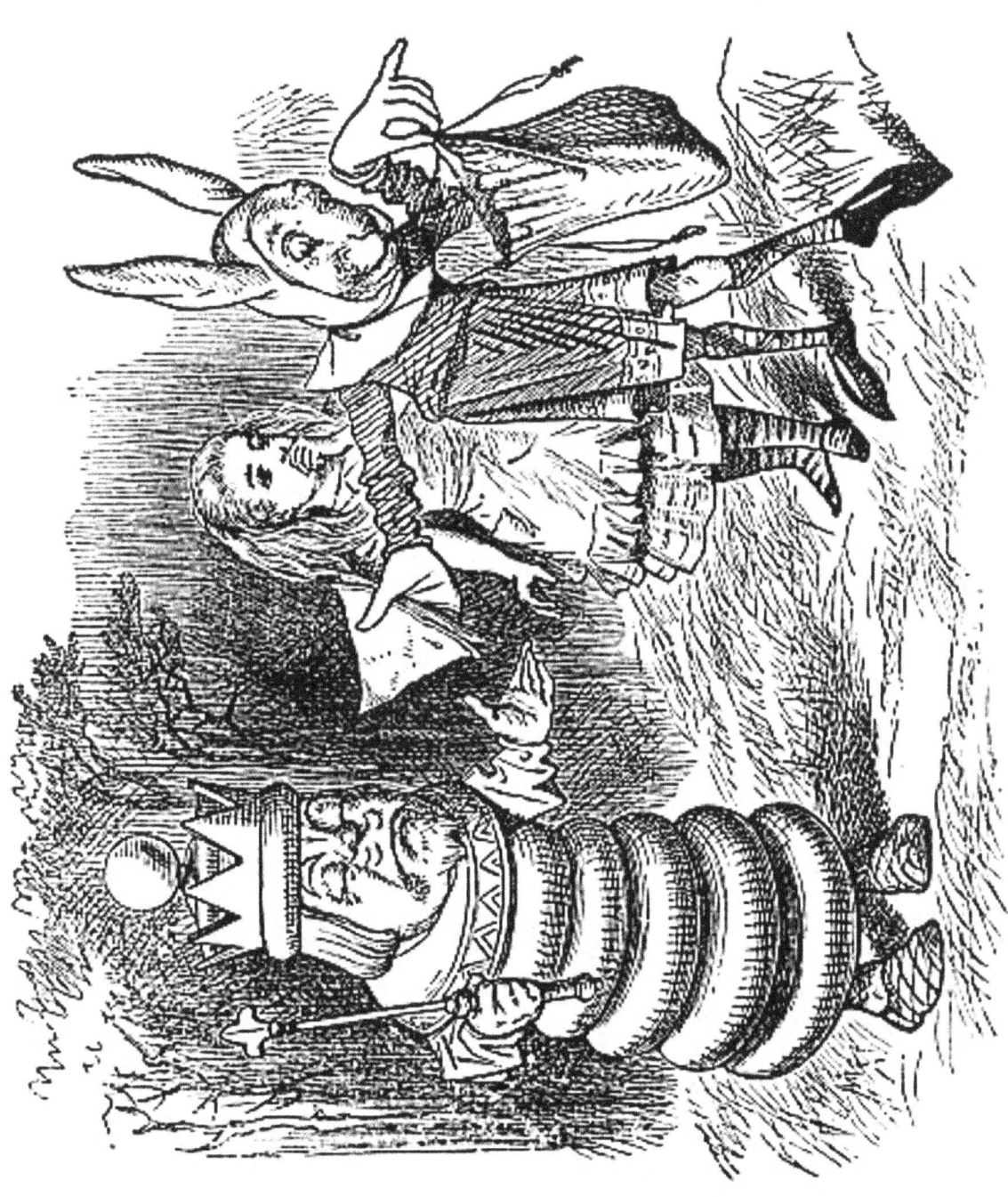

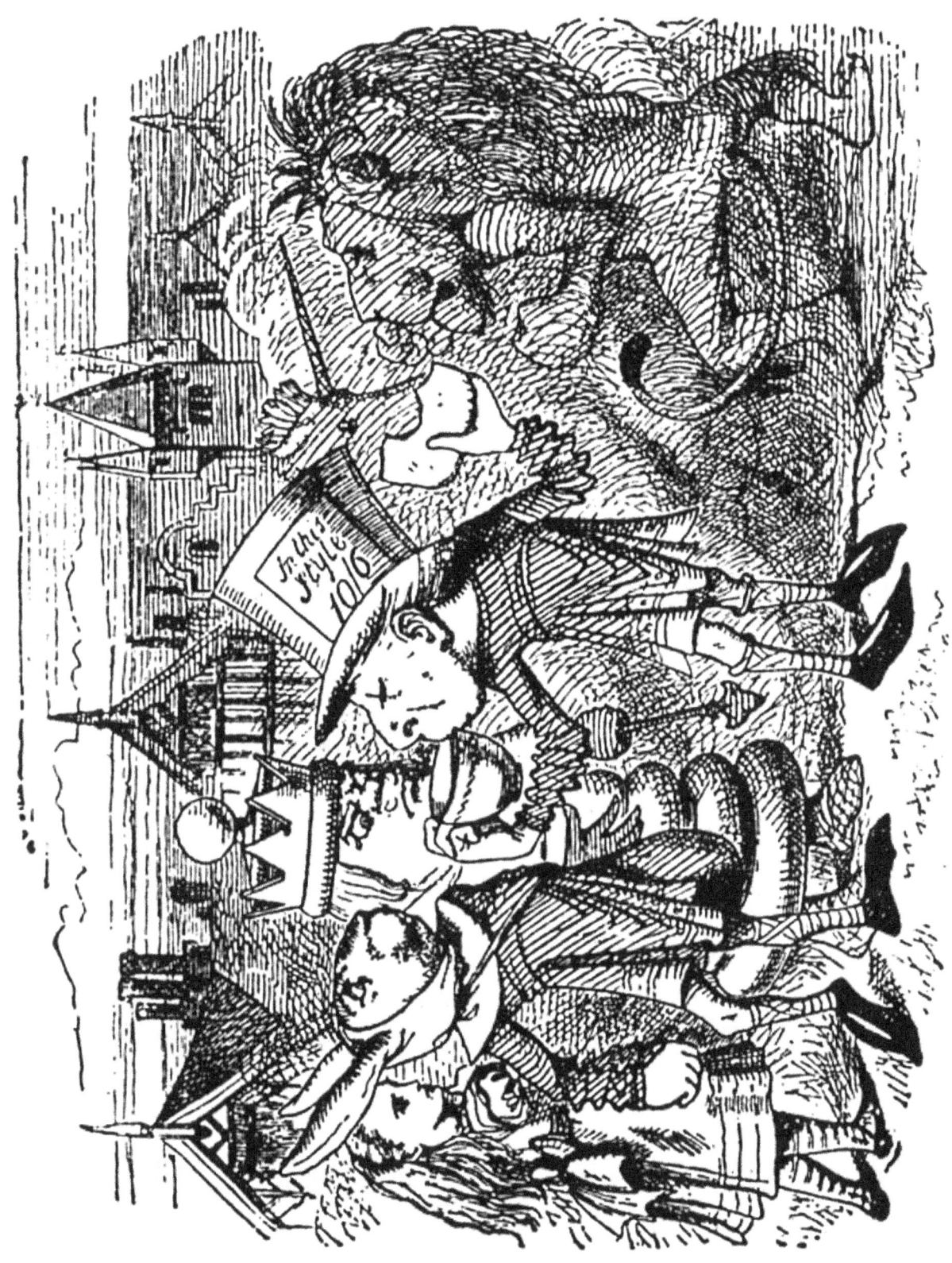

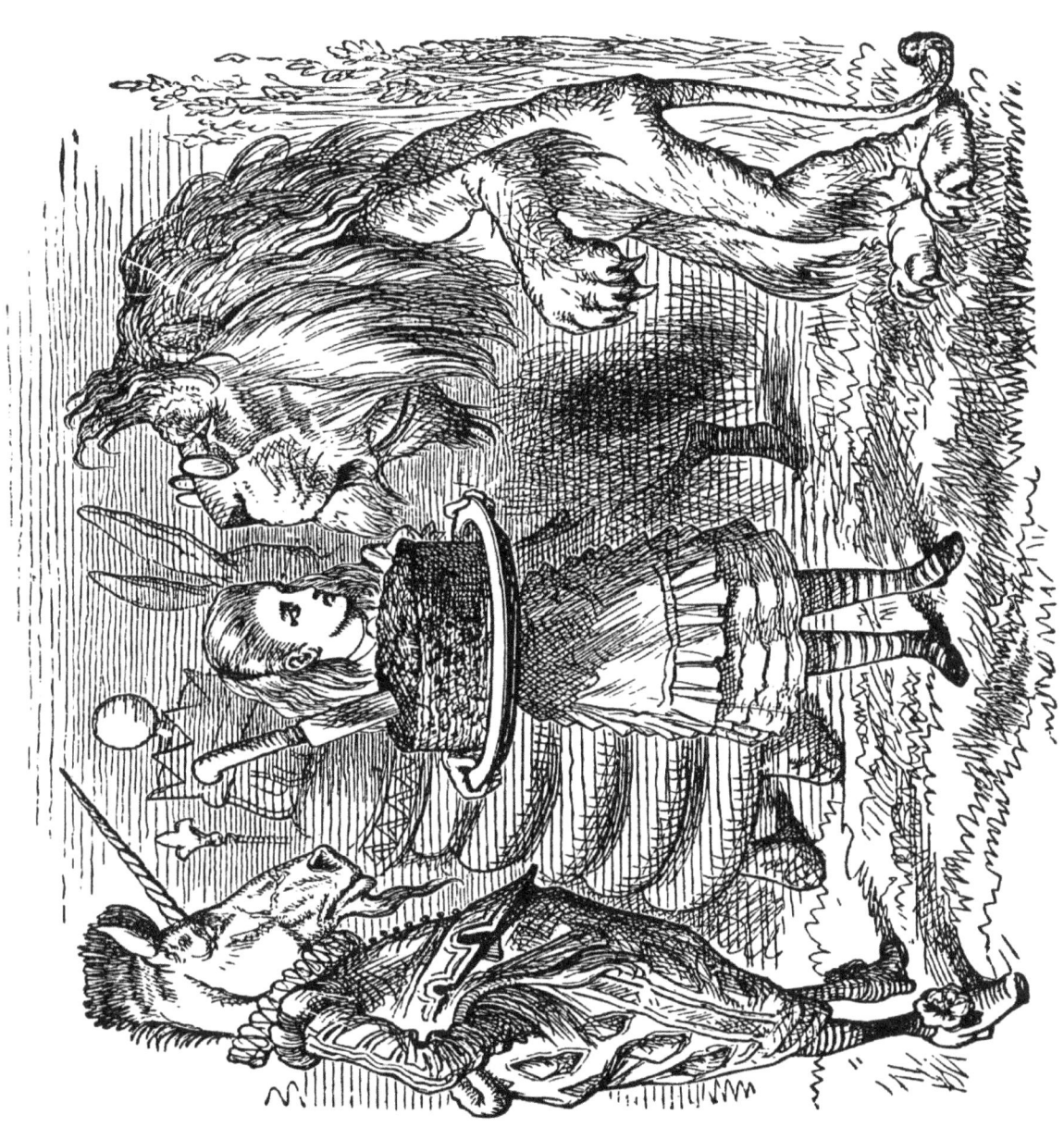

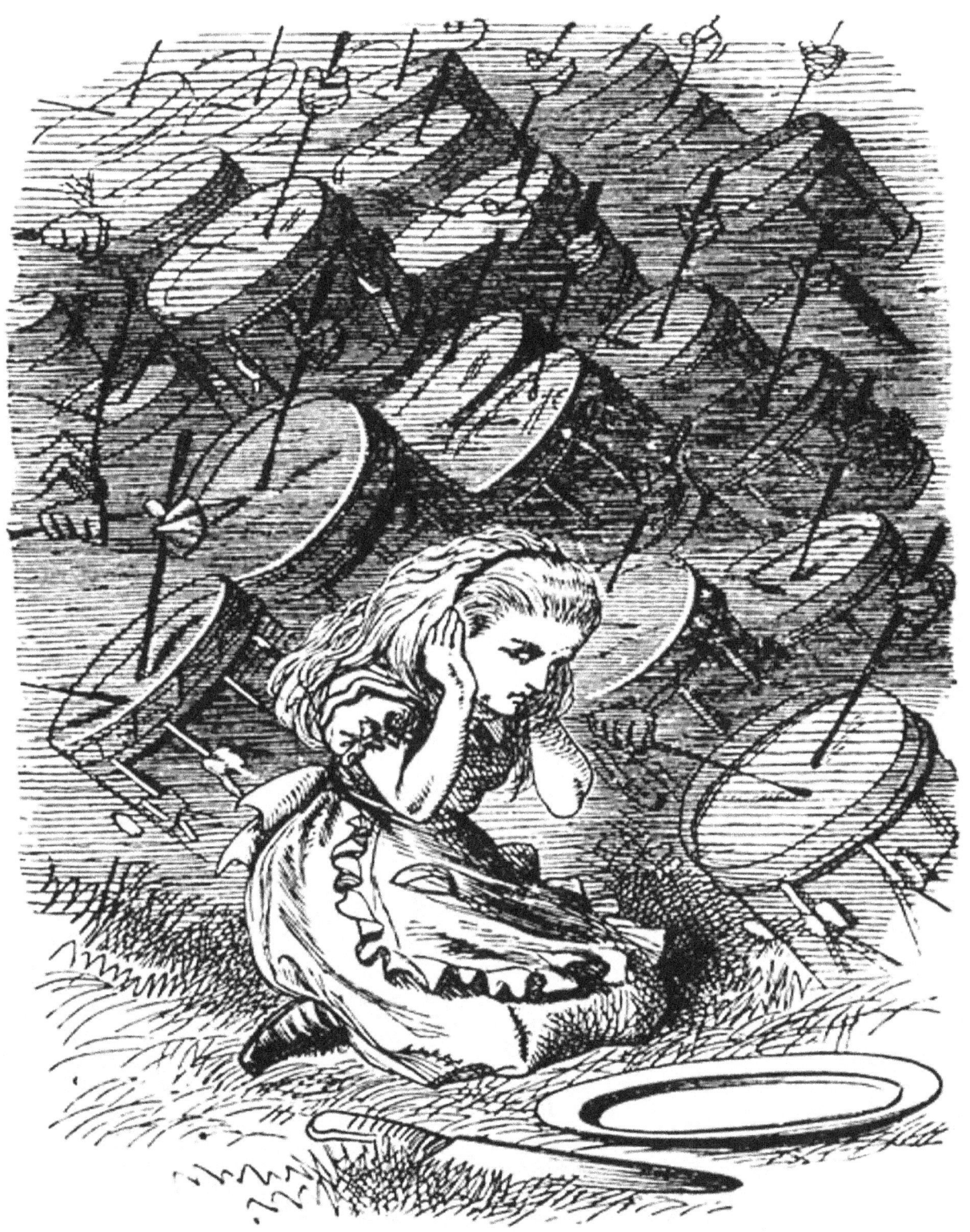

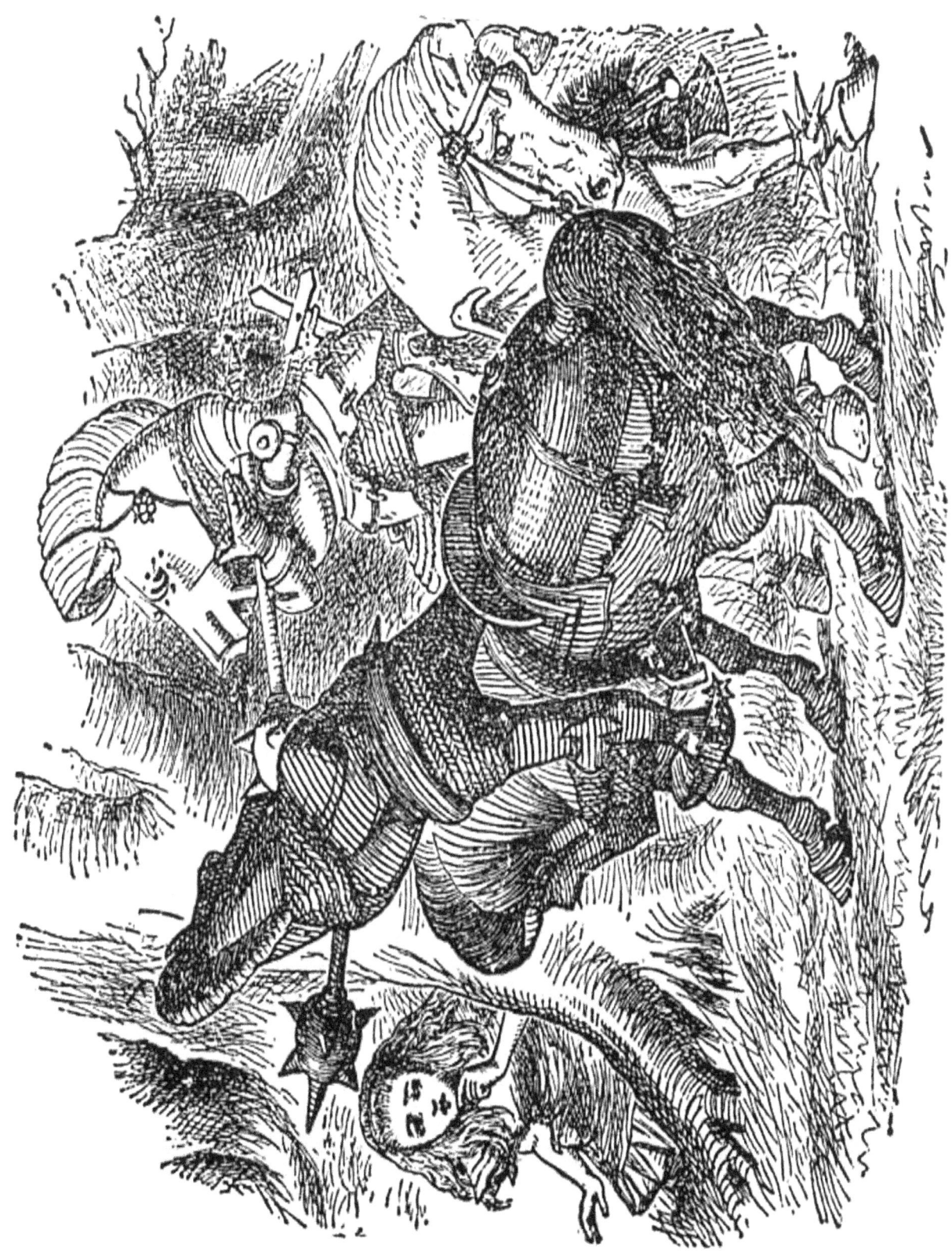

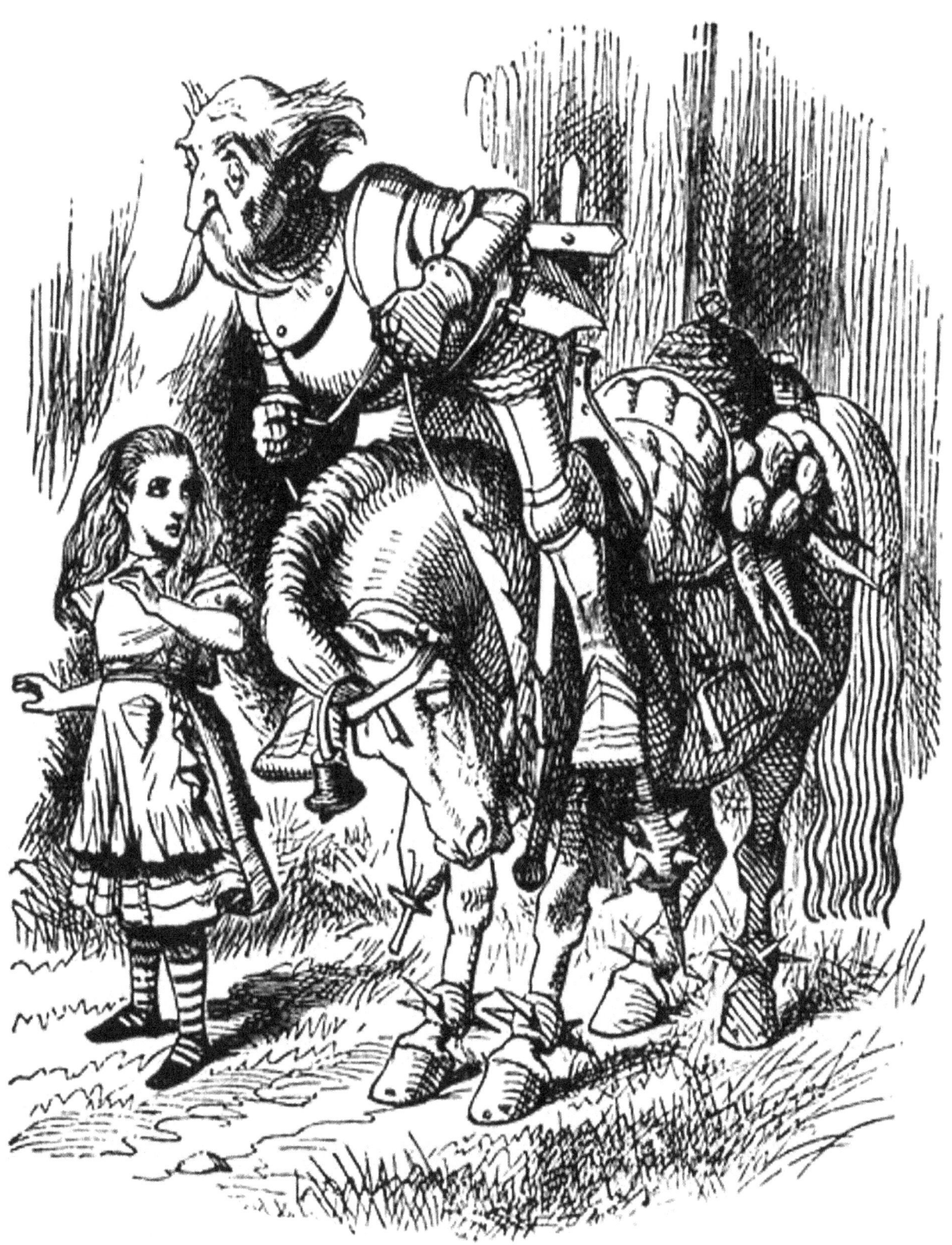

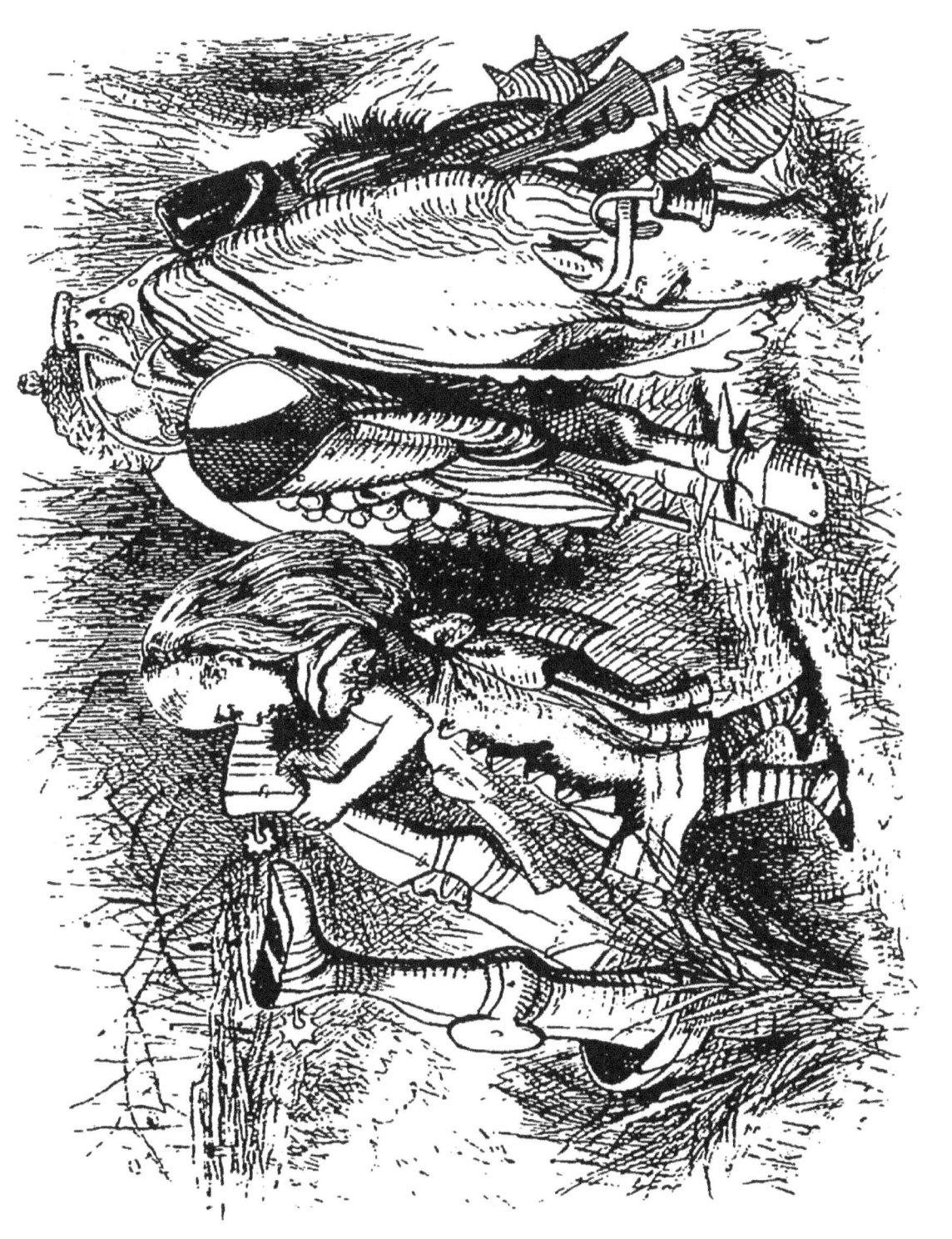

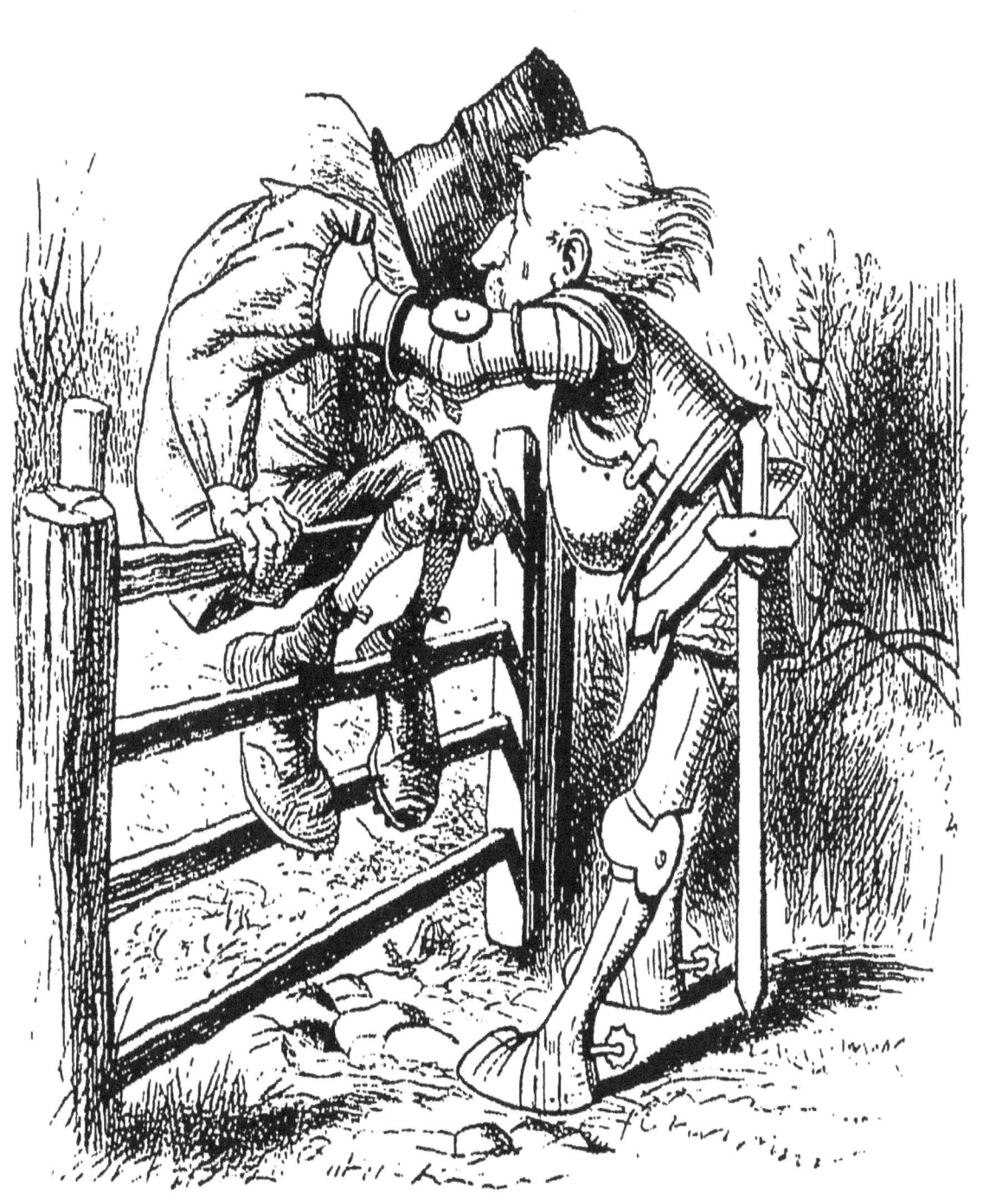

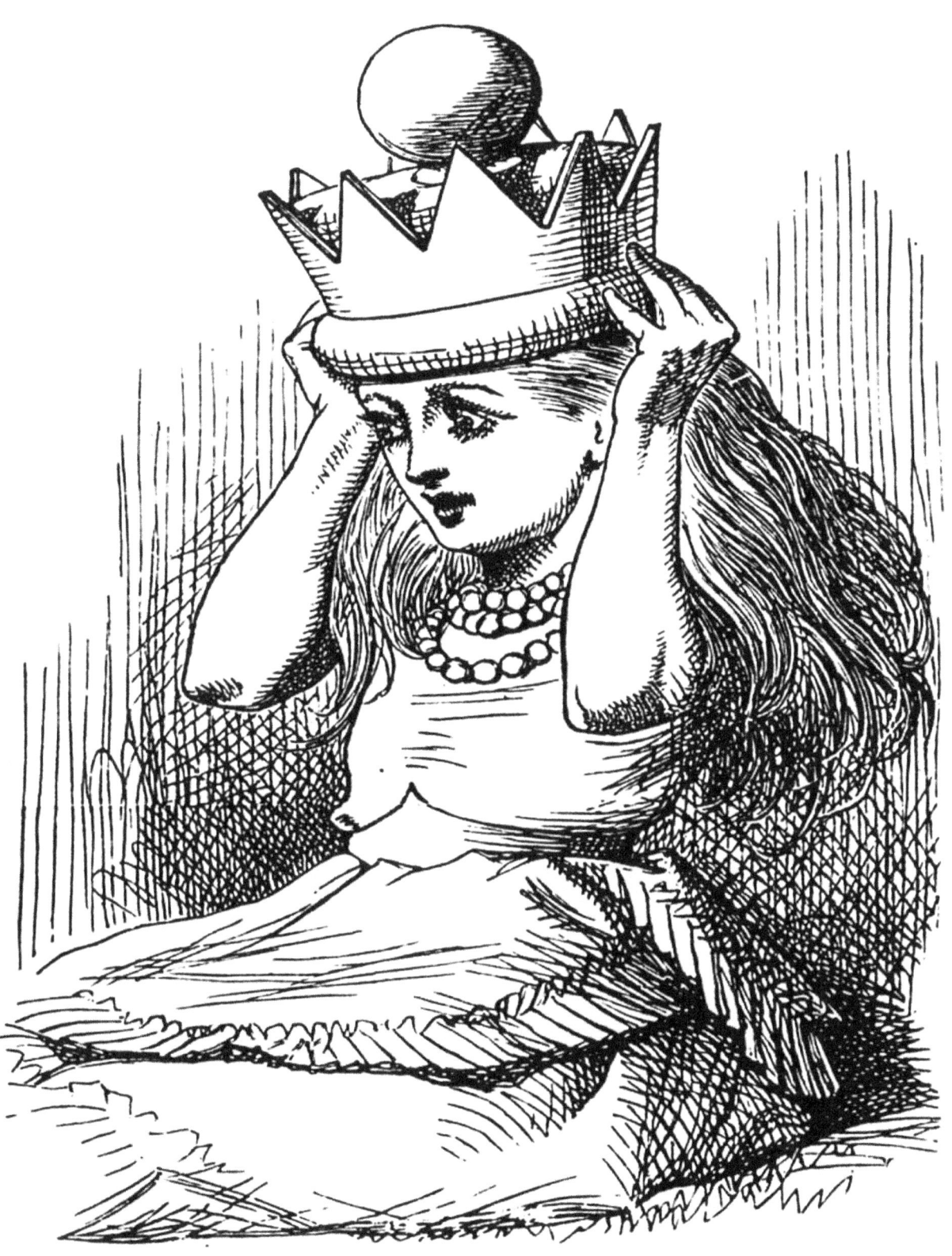

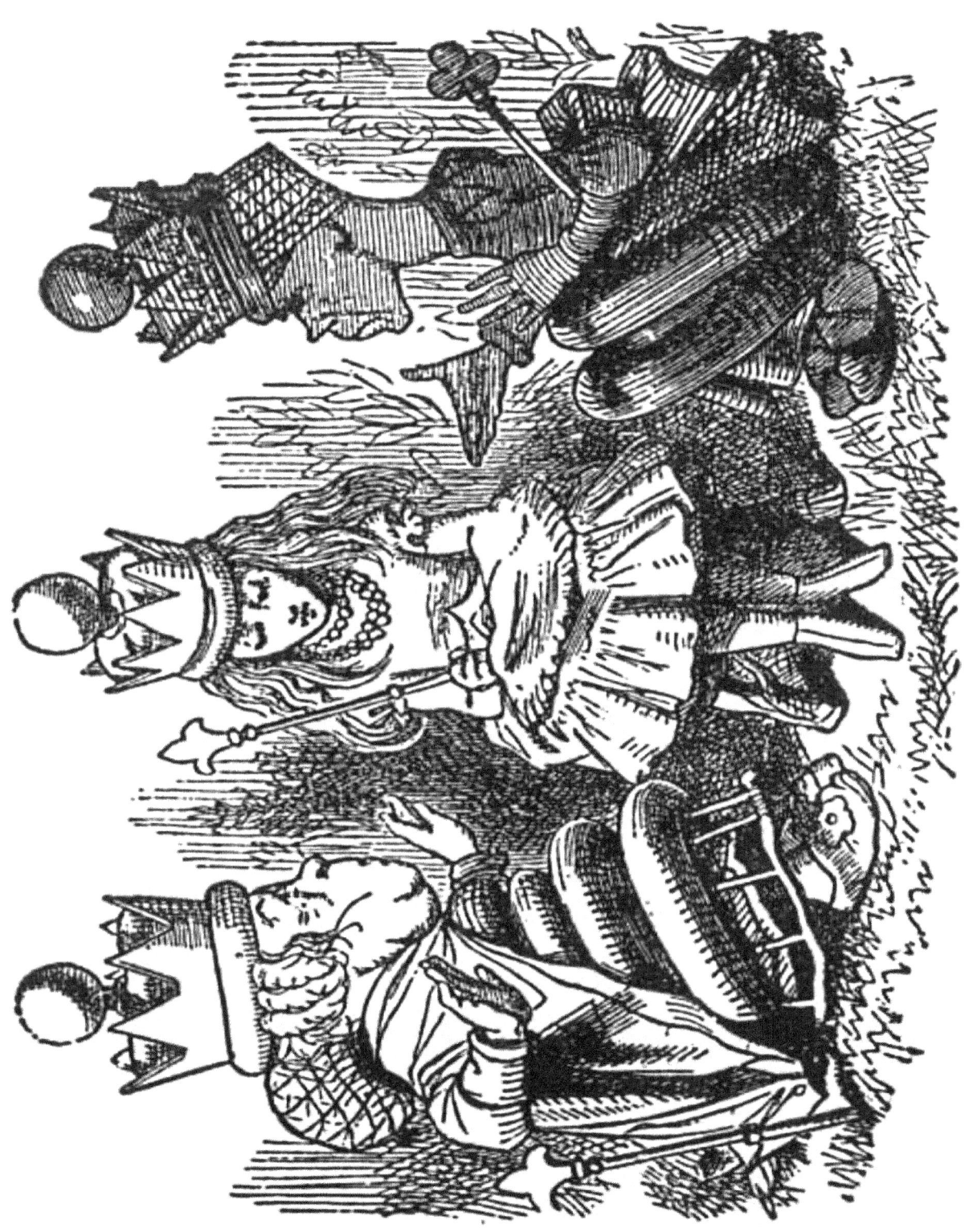

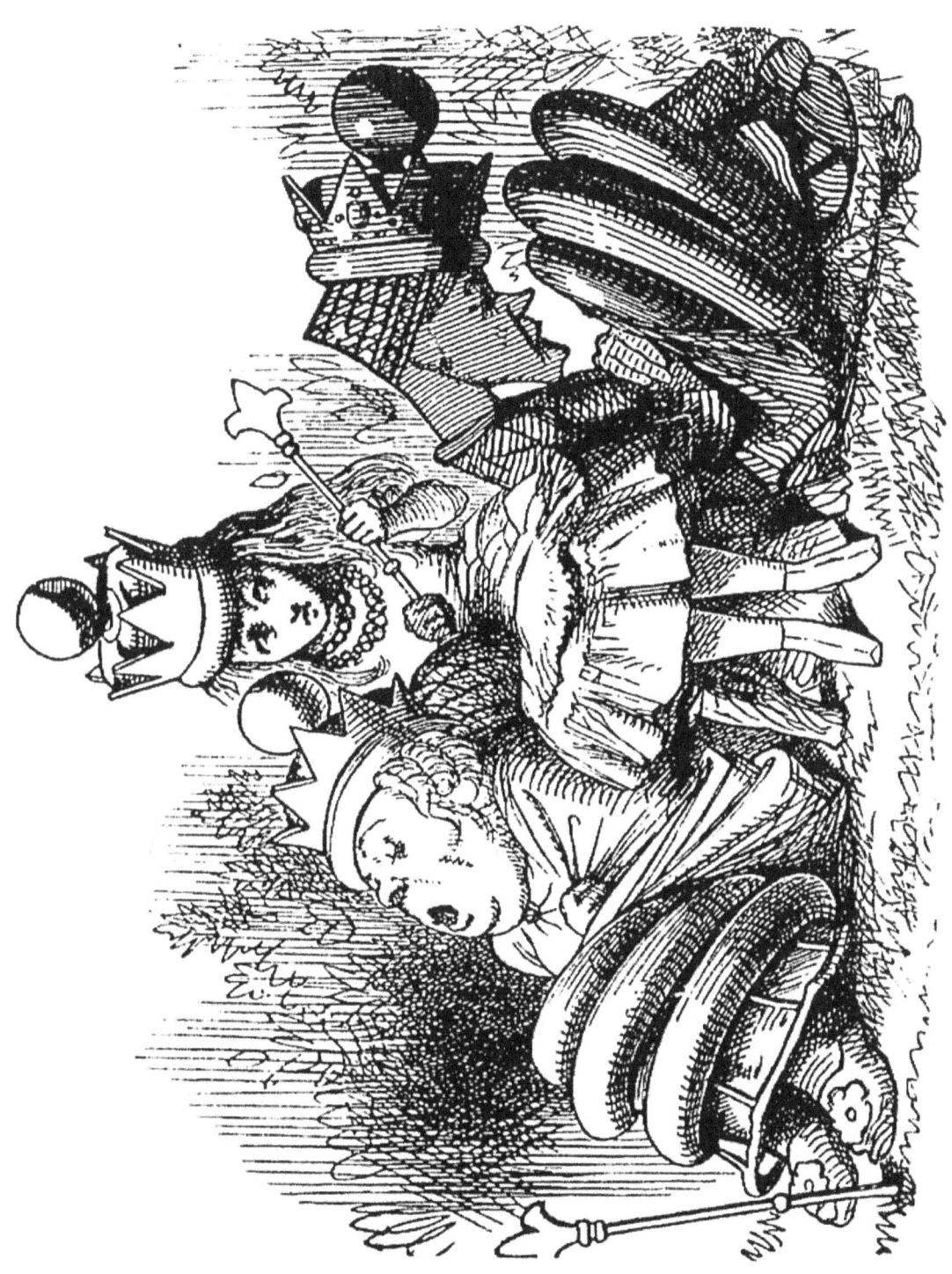

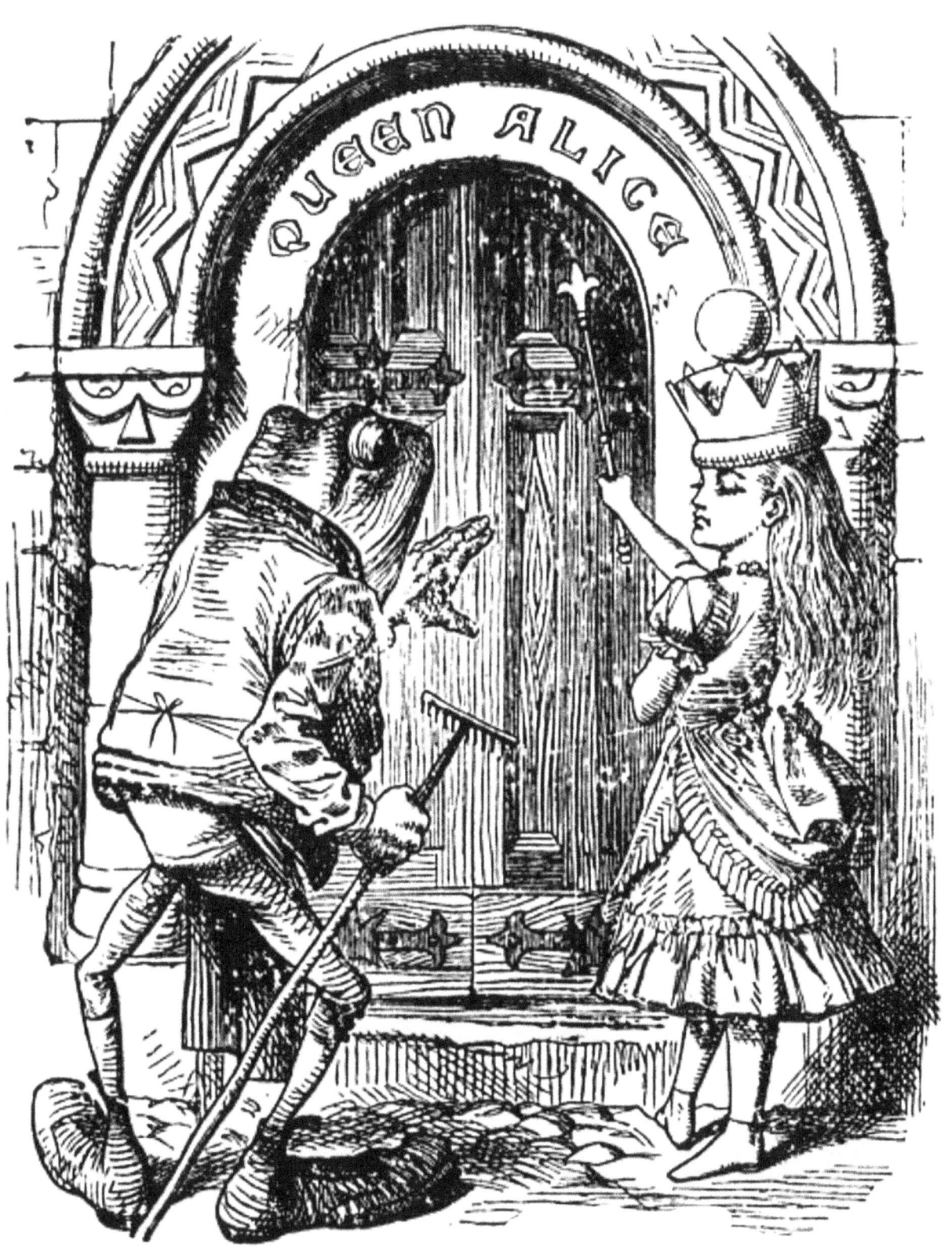

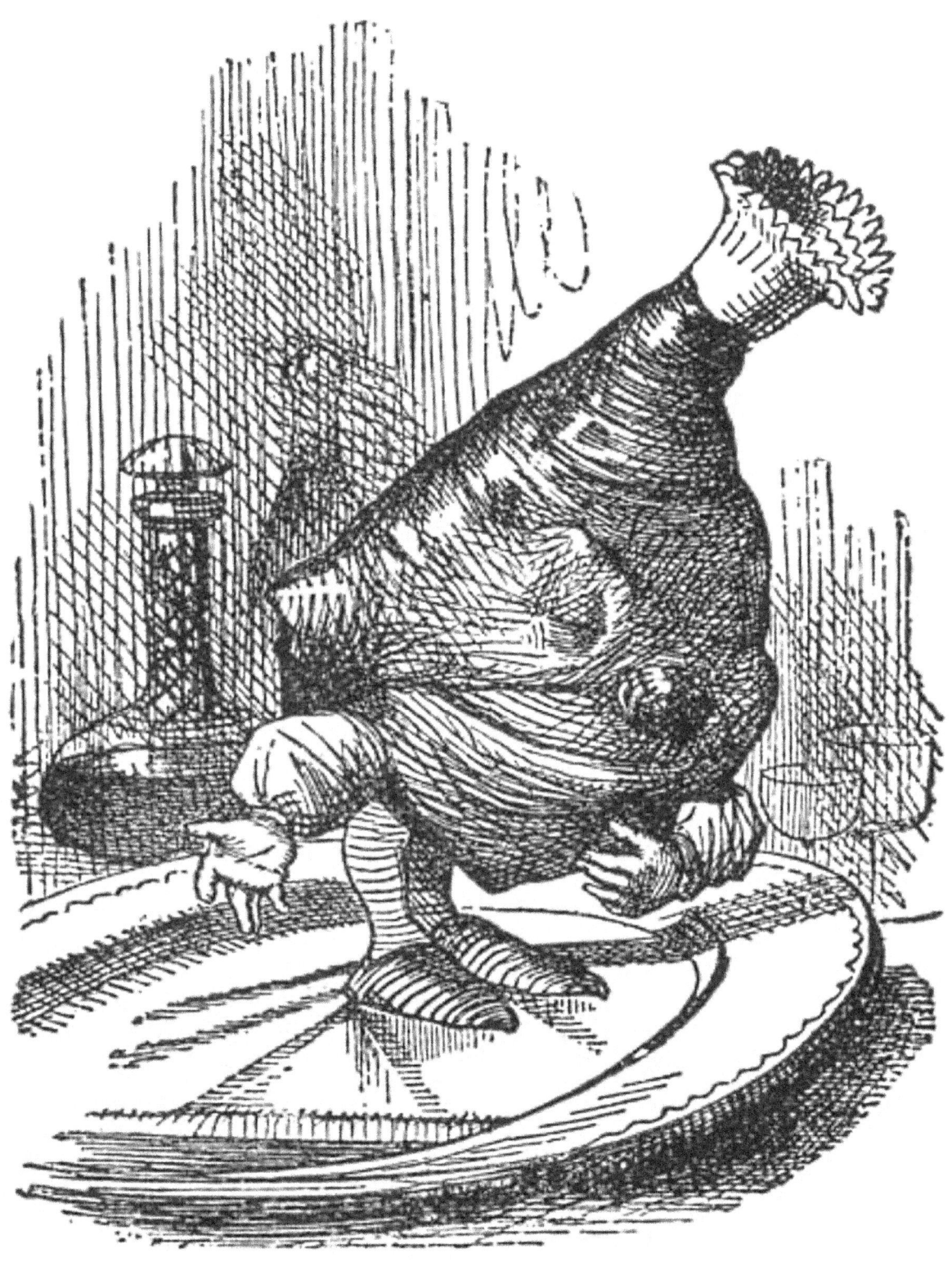

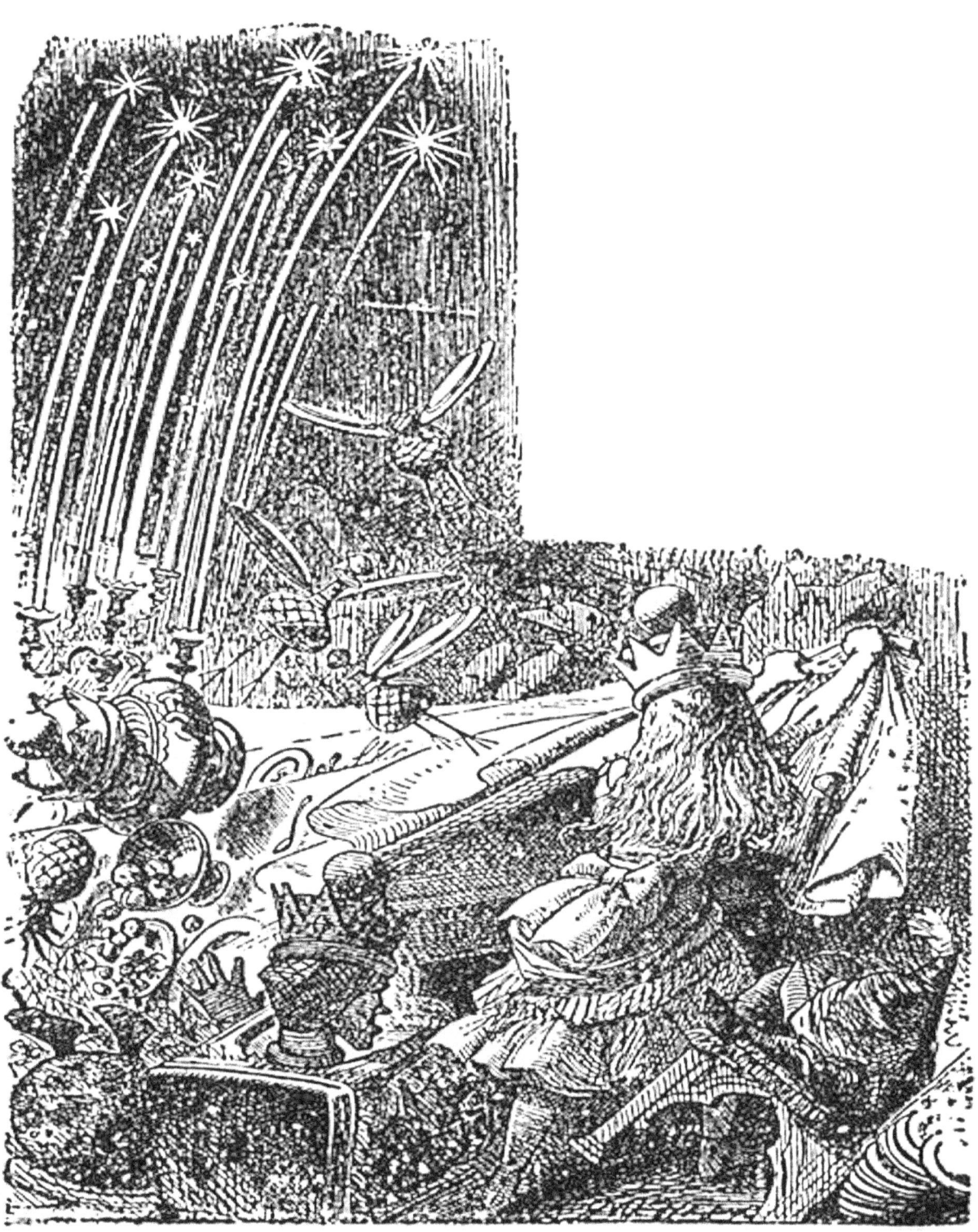

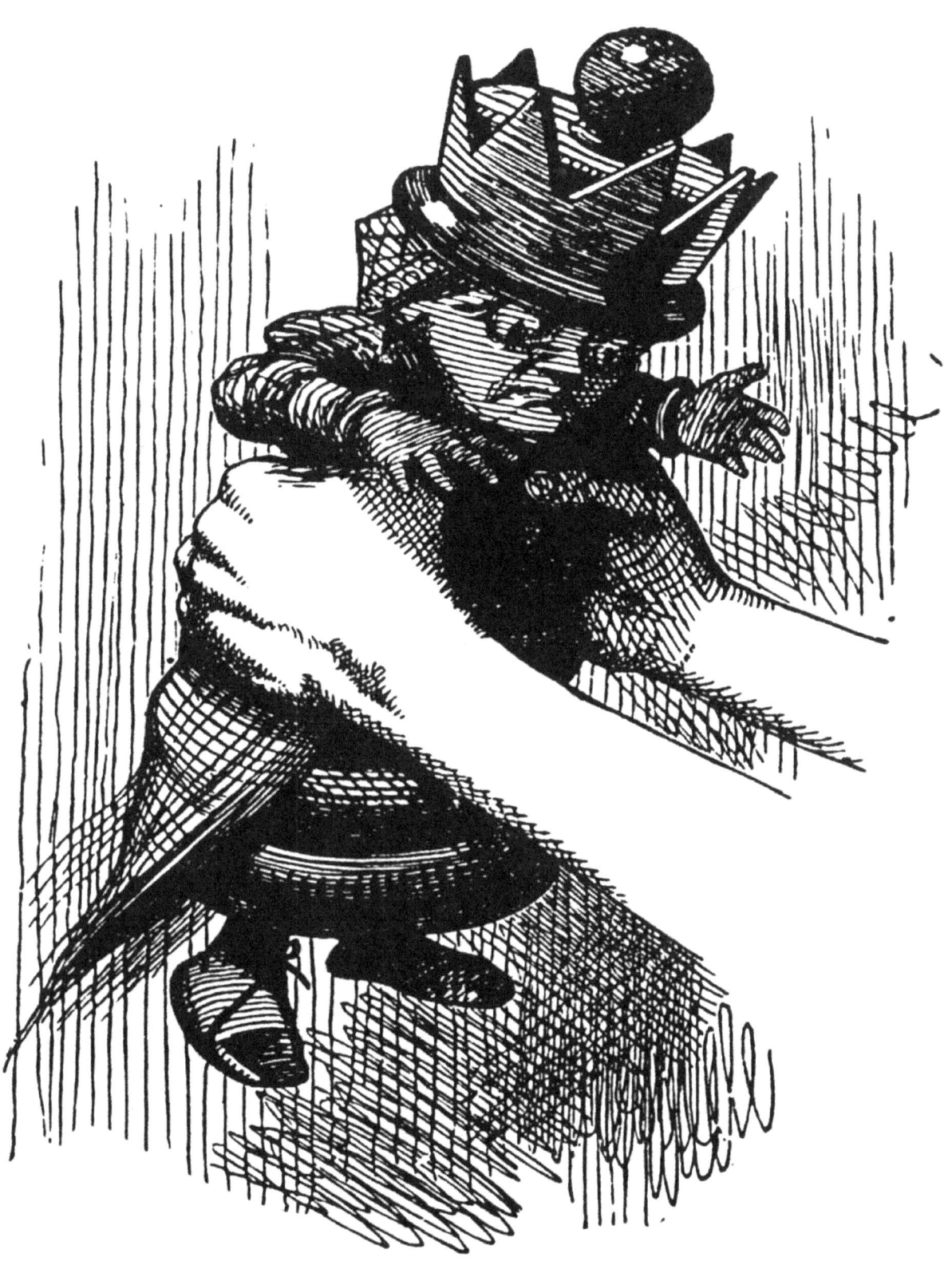

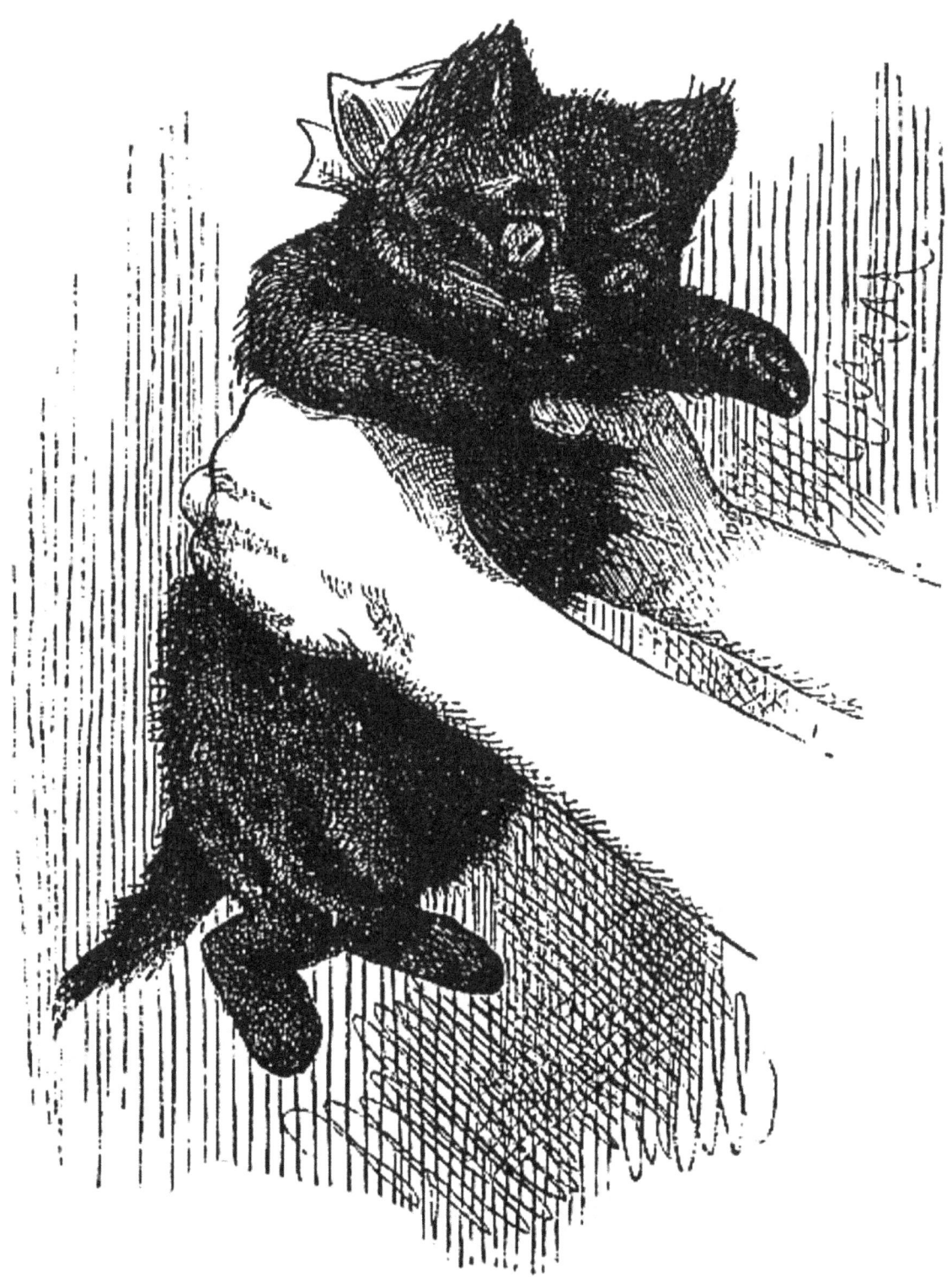

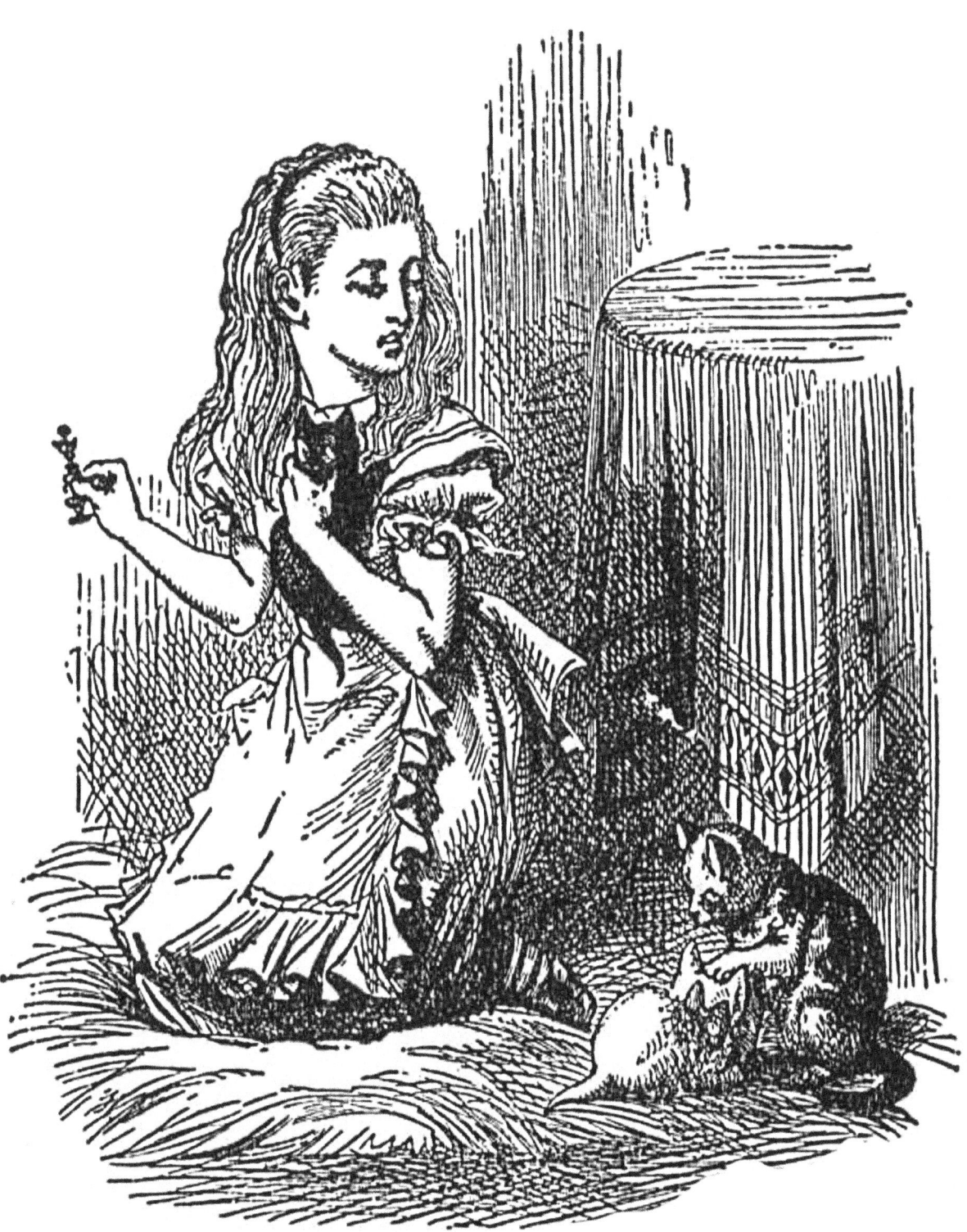

Acknowledgement

Through the Looking Glass and what Alice found there. This is an 1871 novel written by English author Charles Lutwidge Dodgson under the pseudonym Lewis Carroll. It is a sequel to Alice's adventures in Wonderland (1865). Set six months later than the earlier book, Alice again enters a fantastical world, this time by climbing through a mirror into a world that she can see beyond it.

The forty plus book illustrations in this fifth addition series of Grown-Up Coloring Books is the original art of Sir John Tenniel. English Golden Age Illustrator (1820- 1941). This is the artist who originally illustrated both Lewis Carrol's Alice's Adventures in Wonderland and the illustrations contained in this book titled Through the Looking Glass.

Celebrating the 149th anniversary of Alice's Adventures Through the Looking Glass comes this richly illustrated Adult Coloring Book. So now, it is time for you to begin your coloring journey and release your creative abilities upon Tweedledee, Red Queen, White Knight and Jabberwock to say nothing of the immortal young Alice and others. Have fun and enjoy!

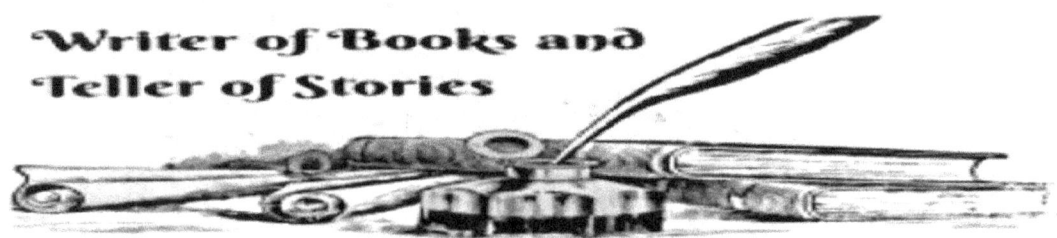

Writer of Books and Teller of Stories

RonaldHudkins.com

Book Review

I appreciate you coloring the line drawings and enjoying the coloring materials contained in this book. Please, if you liked and enjoyed the book take a spare moment to provide a review. It would be a great help if you could post this review to Amazon and let other potential colorers and readers know why you liked it.

This book, as well as, all my other fiction and nonfiction works in their various formats - can be found listed at the following web address; http://www.amazon.com/ . Go into books and type in Ronald E. Hudkins for my complete inventory of works.

Thank you so very much!

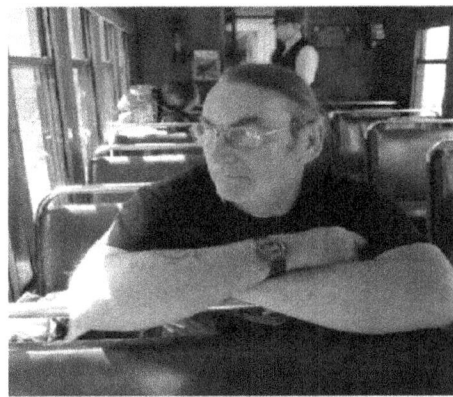

Sincerely

Ronald E. Hudkins

Ronald E. Hudkins

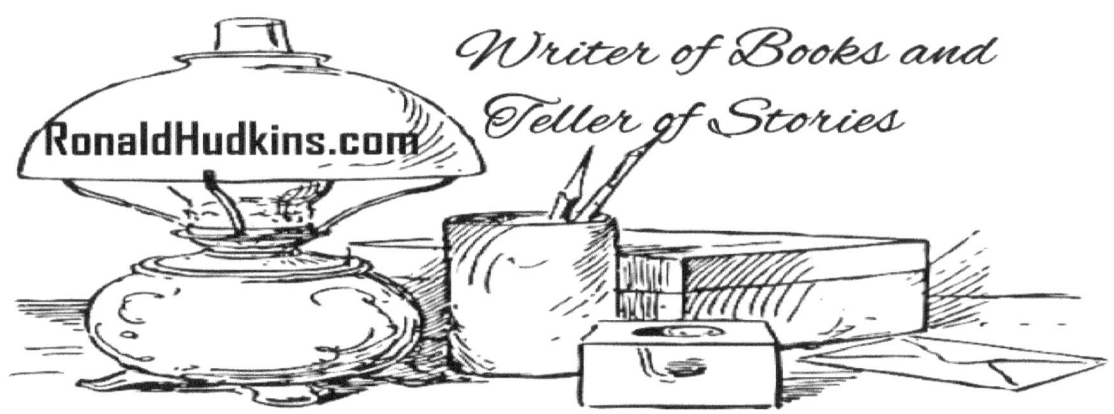